Lessons from My Father

TRUNNIS GOGGINS II

Published By: Veritas Publishing House/Karrpa Imprint

Library of Congress Cataloging-in-Publication Data has been applied for

ISBN: 979-8-9945412-3-4

PRINTED IN THE UNITED STATES OF AMERICA

Disclaimer

The experiences described in this book are based on real events and lived experiences. To protect the privacy and confidentiality of individuals involved, certain names, identifying details, locations, timelines, and circumstances have been changed, omitted, or generalized. In some instances, descriptions may represent composite portrayals created for the purpose of preserving anonymity. These modifications have been made without intent to misrepresent events and do not alter the essential truth or purpose of the stories. Any resemblance to actual persons or events beyond what is intentionally disclosed is coincidental.

Trunnis Goggins and Trunnis Goggins II

Table of Contents

Chapter 1: *Lessons From a Final Journey* 7

Chapter 2: *A New Era of Understanding* 22

Chapter 3: *A Dose of Reality* 40

Chapter 4: *You and I* 62

Chapter 5: *One Big Happy Family* 87

Chapter 6: *1983 - The Year That Changed Everything* 966

Chapter 7: *You Do You* 12121

Chapter 8: *Culture Shock* 14141

Chapter 9: *Am I Not "We"* 15353

Chapter 10: *I am Trunnis Goggins* 17373

Chapter 11: *I am Trunnis Goggins II* 18686

Chapter 12: *The Dark Ages: Freedom, Disorder,
and Personal Parallel* 204

Chapter 13: *Califormia Dreaming* 215

Chapter 14: *Out of the Ashes* 229

Chapter 15: *We good? Yeah, We Good* 251

Chapter 16: *The Reckoning* 265

Chapter 17: *The Tape Recorder in My Head* 281

Afterword: *The Hidden Faces of Domestic Violence* 296

Chapter 1

Lessons From a Final Journey

It was August 2013. I was sitting at my desk at the now-defunct Harrison College, talking with a student who was struggling to stay on track for graduation. My focus was entirely on helping them navigate their challenges when my cell phone rang. I glanced at the caller ID and saw my father's name.

My father and I had been estranged for nearly nine months. Our relationship had deteriorated after years of conflict and unnecessary stress—stress that had affected not only me, but my entire family. For decades, he had a way of creating turmoil out of the smallest situations, and I eventually reached a point where I could no longer continue the cycle. At that time, I didn't know how to manage stress in a healthy way; instead, I simply removed myself from it. As a result, I stopped communicating with him except for brief holiday messages or the occasional courtesy text.

Despite our distance, I knew he had been in declining health. So when I saw his name on my phone, my first thought was that something terrible had happened—that maybe he was gone. I answered immediately.

His voice was weak, frail in a way I had never heard.

"Boy, I'm dying. I'm sick. You won't call and talk to me. I'm tired of this," he said—and then he abruptly hung up.

Startled, I tried calling back. This time, his wife, Janice, answered. I assumed he had accidentally disconnected the call — perhaps his finger brushed the screen. *"Did Dad hang up on me?"* I asked.

"Yes," she responded plainly.

I ended the call, but I knew right then that something was terribly wrong. About twenty minutes later, Janice texted me: Your dad really wants to see you.

It was an odd invitation, but given my father's personality — stubborn, complicated, and often difficult — I understood. I told her I would come that Friday. It was Wednesday, and I felt obligated to finish my work before leaving. After all, my father had always taught me that work comes first. He even opened his business on the days of both his own father's and mother's funerals. He took pride in that ethic, misguided or not. So, I assumed he would understand my need to finish the week.

Still, the thought of him dying weighed heavily on me. On Thursday, Janice asked if I was truly coming. I reassured her that I was.

I made the decision to travel alone. The last time I brought my family, the experience had not gone well. In hindsight, going by myself was the right choice — this was a moment meant for only my father and me.

I drove nine hours from Indianapolis, Indiana to Niagara-on-the-Lake, Ontario. The entire drive I rehearsed what I would say to him. I imagined a firm, necessary, father-to-son conversation — one in which I would finally express everything I had carried for forty-two years. I even booked a hotel room just in case the encounter fell apart.

When I reached Detroit and approached the Ambassador Bridge, the Canadian border officer asked for the purpose of my visit. *"I've got to see my father,"* I replied. Something in my voice must have revealed the gravity of the moment—she asked nothing else and simply waved me through.

We had already endured so many meetings that went wrong. There had been a few in my adulthood that went reasonably well—but this one was different from all the others.

I remember pulling into the driveway and walking up to the front door of my father's house. Every step felt heavier than the last. I rang the doorbell, and Janice answered. The way the house was designed, you could see straight from the front door into the dining room and kitchen area. As she opened the door and I greeted her, my eyes immediately drifted down the hallway.

At the end of that hall sat my father.

He was in a wheelchair. His body was swollen. His frame—once so commanding—looked unfamiliar, almost foreign. For a brief moment, my mind struggled to reconcile what my eyes were seeing. This was not the man I knew. This was not the man who once seemed indestructible.

For the first time in my life—at 42 years old and fully aware of mortality—I was confronted with an undeniable truth: my father, the strongest man I had ever known, was a mere mortal.

Janice would later tell me that she saw it immediately. *The shock on your face was evident*, she said. And she was right. There was no hiding it. No emotional armor could have protected me in that moment.

I have not spoken to Janice in quite some time, and it is highly likely that we never will again. There simply isn't a reason to. But I am genuinely grateful that she served as the liaison who ensured that this meeting between my father and me actually took place. In truth, she could have easily drawn a veil—pulled a curtain tight— and permanently kept us apart.

At that time, my father was far more ill than I ever would have imagined. Had this meeting not happened when it did, I might never have seen him again—not truly, not honestly, not in the final form of the man who shaped so much of my life.

And that realization still lingers.

By this time, my father's eyesight was very poor, and the lighting in the house was equally unforgiving. I know he didn't see my face—and in that moment, I was grateful for that. What he couldn't see, I felt in full force. It was a dose of reality I never imagined I would experience in my lifetime.

Almost instantly, everything I had planned to say to him vanished. Every rehearsed line. Every hard-edged, *man-to-man* conversation I thought we needed to have simply dissolved. The stance I had carried with me—the posture of resolve, of confrontation—was gone.

Standing there, I was no longer facing the myth of my father. I was facing a mortal man.

This was the most influential person in my life, and I was being forced to confront a truth I had spent decades avoiding: there would come a time when he would no longer be here. Whatever challenges we endured, whatever benefits we shared, whatever form our relationship took—it was all approaching its conclusion.

And in that moment, none of the unfinished arguments mattered.

The only thing I could do, seeing my father smiling—genuinely happy to see me—was walk toward him and embrace him. No words. No speeches. Just an embrace.

Almost immediately, he asked, *"How was the drive?" "I'm glad you're here."*

I remember telling him it was a great drive, and that I was glad to see him, too. And I meant it—more deeply than I had ever meant anything before.

In that instant, forty-two years of pain, heartbreak, resentment, and misunderstanding lost their weight. None of it seemed important anymore. What mattered was this: the man so many people admired, the man so many others couldn't stand, the man who battled countless opponents—and often won—was nearing the end of his journey.

And he had called on me.

Not to fight.

Not to argue.

But to walk with him—to help him, in his final steps, on his journey toward eternity.

I know that many people have read about my father and, based on those accounts, have already formed their opinions. And to be honest, I understand why. He was not an easy man. He had many shortcomings—real ones—and those shortcomings undeniably affected a lot of people along the way.

But the story does not end there.

Despite his flaws, there were also many successes. There were meaningful accomplishments. There were great feats that cannot be erased, no matter how complicated the man himself may have been.

My father was born on January 19, 1934, in Calhoun County, Alabama—specifically in Anniston. He left Alabama when he was just two years old, in 1936, but that place never truly left him. Still, whenever I mentioned that he was from Alabama, he would quickly shut it down.

"Don't promote that too much," he'd say.

I remember a similar conversation when I lived in Indiana. When I came back and told people I had been living there, he warned me not to broadcast it. He said that letting people know you were from Indiana—or anywhere rural—made you a *"country boy,"* and in the city, country boys got taken advantage of.

As I got older, I came to understand what was really underneath that warning. His reluctance to let people know he was from Anniston wasn't about shame—it was about survival. He didn't want anyone thinking they could get over on him.

My father was a man of the streets. He believed in leverage. He believed in advantage. And he believed—perhaps wrongly—that if people thought he came from a small town in southern Alabama, they might assume he wasn't intelligent.

Nothing could have been further from the truth.

But in the era he grew up in, the South was often associated with simplicity—a quieter, slower, less sophisticated life. And my father had no patience for anything he considered *"simple."* In fact, when he wanted to insult someone, he would simply call them *simple*.

What's ironic is that, as I grew older, I noticed something he never seemed to reconcile: the people who lived simpler lives often carried far less drama, far fewer conflicts, and far fewer emotional scars than he did. Over time, I realized that simplicity—far from being a weakness—can be essential to happiness.

I'm not suggesting people abandon city life. I love the city myself. But I've come to deeply respect those who come from small towns, who live simply, and who are genuinely satisfied with their lives. That kind of peace is not accidental—it's earned.

My father, however, always carried a chip on his shoulder.

He was born into a family of eleven children. He had a brother named Jimmy who died at the age of two. I believe Jimmy was born before my father, and as far as I know, my father never met him. From what little I've heard over the years, I've often wondered whether Jimmy was born with a physical disability—but I will never know for sure. Most of the people who could have answered those questions have long since passed.

From the age of two onward, my father grew up in Buffalo, New York, in a household that was—at best—unusual. I hesitate to call it chaotic, but it was certainly far from calm. He had seven sisters and three brothers, and based on the stories I heard from my aunts, uncles, and my father himself, their childhood was anything but idyllic.

It was a life marked by hard work, strict discipline, and deeply rooted religious tradition. Order was expected. Obedience was enforced. There was little room for softness.

As my father grew older, he rejected much of that tradition—but its imprint never left him. The discipline, the rigidity, the fight to rise above where he came from—all of it followed him into adulthood and shaped the man the world would eventually meet.

And perhaps, in many ways, shaped the man I would spend my life trying to understand.

My father loved women.

From a very young age, he would share stories with me—often with a grin—about being chased home by women because he was always *"playing around."* He clearly enjoyed telling those stories. There was pride in them, amusement too, as if they were badges of honor from a life lived loudly and unapologetically.

He talked about the cars he bought as a teenager—cars he purchased with his own money. He was proud of that fact, and rightly so. My father was a hard worker, even in his youth. He'd laugh as he told me about loading those cars up with women, making it clear that other guys weren't welcome. Those stories delighted him, and he shared them freely with me, almost as lessons in confidence, dominance, and status.

That love for women didn't fade with time. It followed him throughout his life, and you'll hear many stories in this book that reflect that truth. Some are entertaining, some complicated, and some painful—but they are all honest.

One thing I will always give my father credit for is his work ethic.

He graduated from Fosdick-Masten High School in Buffalo, New York, and he was proud to say that he left home at the age of twenty. Even before that, he had been working for years. He often told me that he started working at the age of nine, plucking chickens at a chicken factory in Buffalo. Whether times demanded it or ambition drove it, my father learned early that survival required effort.

He later worked at a Coca-Cola bottling plant. Eventually, he saved enough money to buy trucks—his own trucks. Those trucks became the foundation of a business. Before long, he owned four Coca-Cola delivery trucks, each one a symbol of upward momentum.

It was on one of his delivery routes that he first noticed a skating rink at the corner of Main and Riley in Buffalo. He saw opportunity where others saw recreation. Through relentless effort, he managed to acquire that building. When it eventually proved too small for his vision, he did something bigger—something bolder.

He purchased an old car garage.

The garage was enormous, and it sat at Main and Ferry. He relocated the skating rink there, transforming that space into what would become a Buffalo institution. That building remained the home of his skating rink business until his death in 2013.

But he didn't stop there.

In addition to the skating rink, my father owned nightclubs, businesses in multiple states, and bowling alleys—you name it. He was always looking for the next move, always trying to stay one step ahead. Rest was not in his vocabulary. Expansion was.

My father also married young. At twenty years old, he entered his first marriage. It didn't last. From that marriage came four daughters—my half-sisters. Their presence, like many things in my father's life, added layers of complexity that would echo for decades.

This was the man my father was: charismatic, driven, flawed, ambitious, excessive, and tireless. He built much. He broke some things, too. And both truths must be told if this story is going to be honest.

My father met my mother in 1969. They remained together—on and off—until 1983. After the release of my brother's book, we are often asked difficult questions. My mother is asked, *Why did you stay?* I am asked, *Why did you go back?*

The truth is, like most real-life stories, this one is not black and white. Life rarely is. Too many variables are at play. Too many moments, too many emotions, too many small decisions that quietly shape the outcome.

What I will say—without hesitation—is that my mother did an outstanding job of trying to establish a family.

I was born in 1971. I was my father's first son, and I was named after him. From a very early age, my mother intentionally fostered a connection between my father and me. She would place me in the bathroom doorway while my father got ready for work. I would sit there, watching him, listening to him talk. At that age, I had no idea what he was saying—but it didn't matter. What mattered was presence.

Connection was being built.

When I was around five years old, my father would call down from the stairwell as he came downstairs. That was my cue. I would run and announce to everyone, *"A star's coming down the stairs!"* That was our ritual—every single day. I would pretend to brush off his suit, straighten him up, and then walk him to his car like a proud escort.

Before he got into the car, he would always hike a football to me. I loved that. It wasn't just a throw—it was a moment. A small exchange that said, *I see you.*

In the summertime, when I was riding my Big Wheel up and down the street, my mother made sure I was outside when my father came home from work. Later, when I graduated to a bike, I was allowed to ride only as far as the next-door neighbor's house. I remember pedaling alongside my father's car as he pulled into the driveway, racing him as if it were the most important competition of my life.

My mother worked tirelessly to create the *semblance* of a normal family.

But we were not a normal family.

From the moment I was born, a bond formed between my father and me. My mother believed in what she called the natural order of things—that a father and his son should be close. And she did everything she could to make that happen.

Looking back now, it almost feels like a scientific experiment.

Two subjects.

Same house.

Same parents.

One was me.

The other was my brother.

By the time my brother was born, my mother had already lived through things she didn't anticipate. The deliberate efforts she made to bond my father and me—she did not repeat in the same way with my brother. The shared rituals, the daily moments, the intentional proximity—they simply weren't there.

That was likely a protection mechanism.

And because of that, the memories I have with my father are not the memories my brother has. We were exposed to different stimuli. We were placed in different emotional environments. And as a result, we developed different responses.

So when people ask why my reactions were different from my brother's—why we processed the same man in different ways—the answer is simple.

We were shaped by different experiences.

Same father.

Different conditioning.

Different outcomes.

And understanding that truth has brought me more clarity— and more peace—than any judgment ever could.

I have always wanted to write a book about my father.

Not to defend him. Not to condemn him. But to explain him.

He was a significant influence in the city of Buffalo, and more importantly, he was the single greatest influence on the man I eventually became. The lessons I learned from him came from both his strengths and his failures—his positive actions and his deeply flawed ones. And I carry both with me.

I am unashamedly proud to call Trunnis Goggins my father.

This book is not *my side of the story*. It is simply my interpretation of a complicated man and an even more complicated time.

Was my father difficult? Yes.

Did he force us—my brother included—to work long hours?

Yes.

Did he treat my mother with respect? Absolutely not.

That last truth is the hardest for me to reconcile. Even now, I struggle to understand how the man who showed me affection, guidance, and pride could treat my mother in ways that were so fundamentally wrong. Holding those two realities in the same space is uncomfortable—but honesty demands it.

My mother once told me that she had seen her father cry only a few times in her life. One of those times was when she went back to my father.

As a father myself, I can tell you without hesitation: I would have done far more than cry. I would never allow anyone to treat my daughter that way. But that was a different era—one shaped by norms, expectations, and family dynamics that people in the 21st century often struggle to comprehend.

It was a time of transition.

A time when silence was mistaken for strength.

When endurance was confused with loyalty.

When roles were rigid, and accountability was uneven.

The world learned many painful lessons during that period—lessons that should never be forgotten and a version of society that should never return.

This book exists not to rewrite history, but to understand it.

It will answer many questions—some comfortable, some not. And it will share lessons born from both triumph and failure. Lessons that shaped not only me, but a family, a community, and a generation navigating a world in the middle of profound change.

This is not a story of absolution.

It is a story of truth.

And sometimes, truth is the greatest inheritance a father can leave behind.

Chapter 2

A New Era of Understanding

The drive from Indianapolis to Niagara-on-the-Lake was absolutely worth it. And in case you were wondering, yes—I canceled the hotel. I spent the night at my father's house instead.

The next morning, Janice had to go to Skateland. It was Saturday, and like every Saturday for more than fifty years, people needed to skate. That was non-negotiable. Her leaving for work meant that I was now responsible for watching my father.

My dad had multiple diagnoses. Diabetes. Failing eyesight. COPD. He could no longer walk. And he was in constant, significant pain. His body was tired in a way only decades of living hard can produce.

The night before, Janice had asked me to take my father to the bathroom. I helped him in and instinctively went to leave to give him privacy—only to learn very quickly that I wasn't going anywhere. I had to stay in the bathroom until he finished.

That was...awkward.

But something happened in that moment—something that fundamentally changed the scope of this visit. I will absolutely share that moment later in this book. If I shared it now, you might feel like you got what you came for and stop reading. So, for now, just sit tight and keep listening to the story.

Before Janice left for work that morning, she gave me very detailed instructions on how to care for my father. I should probably admit something here: I am *not* good with medical stuff. As she was explaining medications, schedules, and contingencies, my internal dialogue was focused on one very specific question—

Is 911 the emergency number in Canada too?

I knew emergency numbers changed from country to country, and I kept reassuring myself that if things went sideways, I at least knew how to dial for help. I can say this with confidence: if anything had gotten even *slightly* out of hand, I would have hit those numbers with Olympic-level speed.

And then it was just the two of us.

The television was on, but my father also had music playing softly in the background. Music had always been a major part of his life. He loved the blues. He loved jazz—the *old* jazz. Not the newer stuff. Definitely not David Sanborn. That wasn't his speed.

That morning, we were listening to a mixed CD of Ray Charles.

And I have to admit—it was perfect.

The room felt still. Heavy.

Two men.

One nearing the end of his journey.

One finally slowing down enough to understand what that meant.

And somewhere between Ray Charles' voice and the quiet hum of the room, I realized this day was going to matter far more than I ever expected.

We sat together and watched CFL football.

I've always loved CFL football, and the reason is simple— my dad took me to a CFL game when I was younger. He used to call it *"funny football."* Canadian money, to him, was *"funny money."* Everything north of the border carried a kind of affectionate suspicion in his mind.

So when it was time to watch funny football, I was ready.

We sat there commenting on how the CFL game seemed faster than the NFL—more motion, more urgency, more chaos in every play. Still, at the end of the day, we both shared the same loyalty. We loved the Buffalo Bills. Always had. We even talked about the Bills game coming up the following Sunday, already looking forward to it like two kids circling a date on the calendar.

It was a genuinely enjoyable Saturday afternoon.

A few times, my dad drifted off to sleep in his chair. Not the deep kind of sleep—just the kind where your head tilts, your breathing changes, and the game keeps playing whether you're awake or not. Each time, he'd wake back up like nothing happened, eyes back on the screen.

Eventually, hunger caught up with me. I got up to prepare some food and asked my dad if he wanted anything. He said no. He probably *was* hungry—but I don't think he trusted my cooking.

Fair enough.

The truth is, I loved *his* cooking. My dad was a great cook. And I think that skill came less from passion and more from necessity. When you live the way he lived—on your own terms, on your own schedule—you either learn to cook well or you go hungry.

Watching him there that afternoon—dozing, waking, joking, critiquing football—I realized how much of who I am was shaped in moments just like this. No speeches. No lessons delivered directly.

Just time.

And sometimes, time is the greatest inheritance a father can give a son.

As I've said before, my father was a very complicated man. And because of that complexity, there were long stretches of his adult life when he was essentially alone. If I'm being honest, I would say my father had *four different families* once he reached adulthood—each one layered on top of the last, each one leaving its own mark.

His first family was with his wife, Dolores. During that marriage, he had four children—my half-sisters. Most of what I know about that family comes from fragmented stories: bits and pieces he shared, and small details I later heard from my sisters themselves.

One story my father told often—and with noticeable bitterness—was how his first wife had the Erie County Sheriff serve him divorce papers *right in the middle of dinner*. He spoke about that moment as if it were a public execution. According to him, the divorce was so brutal that he lost everything financially. Whether that was fully accurate or not, the impact was real. He made a vow that day that he would never allow himself to be that vulnerable again.

That decision would later have consequences—especially for my mother, even though she wouldn't enter the picture for several more years.

In between, there was another woman. Her name was Irene. From what my father told me, she desperately wanted to be with him. But then he met my mother, and everything shifted. I was born shortly after.

My father once told me a story about Irene that I still don't quite know what to do with. He claimed that when I was about two months old, she tried to run my mother and me over with a car. I honestly don't know why he ever shared that story with me. In fact, what disturbed me most wasn't just the story itself—it was the way he told it. There was almost a sense of pride in his voice, as if the chaos somehow validated his importance.

That's not something I would ever be proud of.

I don't know if the story is true. I never will. But true or not, it tells you everything you need to know about the environment—the emotional volatility, the instability, the tension—that surrounded my early life. So yes, the story is fucked up, but it's part of legend now.

That brings us to what I consider my father's second family: my mother, my sisters, and me.

That period was turbulent—there's no softer word for it.

When I was two years old, my sister's mother passed away. My father did not handle her death well at all. I truly believe that unresolved grief turned into anger, and that anger bled into every corner of our household.

At the same time, my father often bragged that I was *"the future of the family."* Looking back, I can see how damaging that was. I don't think he realized—or maybe didn't care—that those words likely fueled resentment toward me from my sisters.

My sisters also hated my mother.

For clarity, my oldest sister moved out of the house when I was very young, so I never really lived with her. The other three did live with us—but their presence was inconsistent.

They often ran away, moved in with their mother's family, then returned for periods of time before leaving again.

Of the sisters who lived with us, two were not particularly kind to me. And that's putting it gently.

This was the emotional landscape of my childhood: fractured families, unresolved grief, misplaced pride, and resentment that had nowhere healthy to go. None of it existed in isolation. Every decision, every word spoken—or left unspoken—rippled outward.

And I was growing up right in the middle of it.

The only thing I was ever guilty of was being born to a different mother.

I did nothing to them. And yet, fifty years later, the same two sisters still treat me with the same level of disdain. Time did not soften it. Distance did not heal it. It simply calcified.

In my younger adult years, I made genuine attempts to reach out to them. I tried to build some form of brother-sister relationship. I extended olive branches that were never accepted. No matter what I did, I couldn't break through the wall they had built.

Eventually, I realized I was wasting my time.

So I stopped trying and moved on. I will describe that realization—and what it cost me—later in this book.

There was, however, one sister who was different. She was kind to me. She still is. To this day, we remain close. We talk about once a month, and out of all my siblings, she is the only one I truly share parts of my life with. That connection has mattered more to me than she probably realizes.

I know my sisters are close to each other. But if you look at all of us collectively, there is no real sense of family unity. I seriously doubt there will ever be a Goggins family reunion organized by my siblings.

My children, for example, don't even know their cousins from my sisters. That wasn't the result of one dramatic decision—it was the product of years of emotional distance and neglect. It was never made a priority. And over time, it simply became normal.

What I do know—without question—is that the household under this second family was deeply toxic.

I remember my father being angry at my sisters.

I remember my sisters being angry at my mother.

I remember my mother trapped in an impossible situation.

And to be honest with you, it was an unfair position from the start. My mother was only seven years older than my oldest sister. To put someone that young into that dynamic—to expect her to manage grief, resentment, discipline, and loyalty—was profoundly irresponsible.

That house was not just tense; it was combustible.

Everyone was reacting. No one was healing. And I was growing up in the middle of it, learning lessons about family, loyalty, and survival that would take decades to fully understand.

Some families fracture loudly.

Others fracture quietly.

Ours did both.

Then there was what I call the third family.

The third family consisted of my father, my mother, me—and then my brother, David. By the time David was born, my sisters had mostly moved out. The youngest was still around from time to time, but the others had largely moved on with their lives. In fact, I have a nephew who is only two months younger than my brother, which tells you just how overlapping and complicated our family timeline really was.

That third family existed from 1975 until 1983.

After that came what I consider my father's fourth family—one that looked very different from the others. This family was my father, Janice, and me. That chapter ran from 1985 until 1989, when I graduated from high school.

That period of my life—those years with Janice—I consider my *only* childhood.

It was during that time that I saw a completely different side of my father. A version of him that, when I try to describe it to other family members, they look at me like I'm speaking a foreign language. They don't recognize the man I'm talking about. They don't understand the experiences I'm referencing.

And again—I'll come back to that later in the book.

Circling back to my father and his cooking, I truly believe the reason he became such a good cook was simple necessity. There's only so much shit a woman is willing to take before she finally decides she's had enough.

And when that happened, they left.

When they did, my father was left to fend for himself. So he learned to cook. And he learned to cook well. Not out of passion or hobby—but out of survival. It was one of the few domestic skills he fully mastered, and like everything else in his life, it came at a cost.

That's the recurring pattern in my father's story: adaptation without reflection. Survival without repair.

And somehow, through all of it, I was still watching—still learning—still becoming the man I would one day have to reckon with myself.

There were a few times in my life when the women in my father's life left, and it was just the two of us. When that happened, my father cooked—because he had to.

I remember one year in high school when my father and I spent Christmas alone together. He cooked the entire meal himself. The reason it was just the two of us? He had managed to piss a woman off—again. But I'll tell you this without hesitation: that Christmas dinner was *really* good. And the gift exchange that year was even better. It was fun, light, and unexpectedly joyful.

The number-one song that Christmas was *"Do They Know It's Christmas?"* And every time I hear that song, I don't think about starving children in Africa. I think about that Christmas—just my dad and me—sitting together, making the best of what we had.

That memory came rushing back as I sat with my father years later, watching CFL football and realizing I was hungry. Since my dad didn't want to eat—and since I've never been a great cook, a fact that remains true to this day—I decided to make myself a sandwich.

When I opened the refrigerator, I saw cotto salami.

I hadn't had it in years. But the sight of that deli meat hit me with a wave of nostalgia. My father *loved* cotto salami. When we lived together back when I was in second grade, he made my lunch every single day. The sandwich was always the same: cotto salami, Miracle Whip, Wonder Bread. And it always came with either two Hostess Ho Hos or a big cookie from Tops Supermarket.

And let me be clear—there is no better cookie than a Tops Supermarket cookie. If a representative from Tops is reading this book, I'm open to sponsorship discussions.

So there I was—42 years old—sitting alone with my father, eating a cotto salami sandwich and watching CFL football. Something I hadn't done since I was seven.

Only this time, the roles were reversed.

Instead of my father watching over me, I was watching over him. His safety now depended on my responsibility. That shift—more than anything else—hit me hard.

What saddened me most wasn't the caregiving. It was the silence.

My father had six children and seventeen grandchildren, yet I was the only one sitting there with him. And I want to be clear—I'm not saying that to shame anyone. My siblings, my nieces, and my nephews all had valid reasons for not being there. And honestly, I believe my father understood that.

Maybe that's why he was so glad to see me.

Not because I was his favorite—but because I was willing to come.

As a father myself, I cannot imagine preparing to leave this earth without my sons and daughters by my side. But life choices, pride, and blind ambition created a family dynamic that made that impossible for him.

And so, in that quiet room—with Ray Charles in the background, CFL football on the television, and a cotto salami sandwich in my hand—I found myself sitting in the middle of a moment shaped by decades of decisions.

Some loving.

Some selfish.

Some irreversible.

And all of them leading right there—to that chair, that sandwich, and that final stretch of time between a father and his son.

The most valuable lesson I took from that weekend—sitting beside my father—was simple and undeniable: make sure your children know that you love them.

What struck me as almost surreal about that time was this—while my father sat in his recliner in Niagara-on-the-Lake, Ontario, resting and quietly contemplating the sum of his life decisions, *everything he had ever created was still moving forward*. My sisters were doing what they had to do. My brother was doing what he had to do. My mother was doing everything she had to do. Life didn't pause just because he had slowed down.

The music was still playing at 33 E. Ferry Street.

Businesses were still running.

People were still skating.

And quite frankly, once the Buffalo Bills finished playing the Carolina Panthers that Sunday, I would have to leave and continue doing what *I* had to do.

Saturday passed without a hitch. My father and I genuinely enjoyed our time together. When Sunday morning arrived, I felt more comfortable caring for him. I finally knew how to do a finger-stick sugar test. I learned how to give insulin. What once felt intimidating now felt manageable.

Then we watched the Bills game.

Ironically, it turned out to be one of the best games of the entire drought era. The starting quarterback that day was E.J. Manuel. The Bills were down in the final minute, and Manuel pulled off a miraculous, game-winning drive. What made the moment unforgettable wasn't just the win—it was what happened next.

E.J. ran straight to the stands and embraced his father.

It was a beautiful moment in sports. Father and son, holding each other, both overcome with emotion. Tears of joy. Pride. Relief. Love.

My father and I looked at each other.

We didn't say a word.

We just smirked.

Goggins men don't show emotion—but we both understood the significance of what we had just witnessed. And we both knew *why* it mattered.

Around five o'clock that evening, Janice came home from Skateland. It was time for me to head back to Indianapolis— back to my family, back to my responsibilities. As I stood up to leave, my father asked a question that caught me off guard.

"When will you be back?"

I looked at him, fully aware that there wouldn't be many more opportunities to answer that question. And without hesitation, I said, *"I'll see you Friday."*

He paused. *"This Friday?"*

"Yes. This Friday."

He smiled. I smiled. Then he said, *"Call me when you get home. You know I can't go to sleep unless I know you're home."*

I remember thinking to myself, *I'm forty-two years old—I can take care of myself.*

And yet… I made sure to call him when I got home.

Today, I'm in my mid-fifties. My children are grown. Some are in the military. Some are working toward advanced terminal degrees. And when they visit me, I tell them the same thing my father told me:

"Make sure you call me when you get home. I can't sleep unless I know you're safe."

On the drive back to Indianapolis, I had seven and a half — maybe nine — hours to think. Mostly, I thought about family.

About choices. About patterns passed down, whether intentionally or not.

As I walked out the door earlier that evening, I said, *"See you Friday."*

My father replied, *"Okay. Love you."*

Goggins men never say that to each other.

But in that moment, I knew — *times had changed*. And so had I.

It was time to reconcile a new era.

Chapter 3

A Dose of Reality

The following Friday, when I came to see my father, it was no longer in Niagara-on-the-Lake, Ontario.

It was at Buffalo General Hospital in Buffalo, New York.

After I returned to Indianapolis from Niagara-on-the-Lake, my sister Marina came to visit my father. While she was there, he suffered a serious medical episode—one severe enough that Janice and Marina had to call 911. He was taken briefly to a hospital in the Niagara region of Canada, but it didn't take long for doctors to determine that he needed more extensive care. The decision was made to transport him across the border to Buffalo.

Marina and I had spoken shortly after I left Niagara-on-the-Lake the first time. I told her plainly that Dad was not doing well at all. She didn't hesitate. She flew from California to Niagara-on-the-Lake almost immediately.

My sister Marina is one of the sweetest people you will ever meet. She endured a great deal of trauma herself growing up, yet she somehow retained an extraordinary ability to see the good in nearly everything. That perspective has always amazed me. She was—and still is—a major influence in my life. I deeply admire her philosophy on life, and I try to incorporate as much of it as I can into my own.

Now, when it comes to politics, Marina and I could not be more different.

She is firmly loyal to one side of the political spectrum. I, on the other hand, find flaws in every corner of the U.S. political system and have developed a fairly cynical view over the years. Even now, she'll ask me a political question knowing full well she's probably not going to agree with my answer.

And yet—that's one of the things I love most about our relationship.

We agree to disagree. And more importantly, we continue to love each other.

We don't talk every day. Hell, we don't even talk every month. But we *think* about each other. And when too much time passes, one of us always picks up the phone and reaches out. There's comfort in that kind of unspoken bond.

So my second visit with my father was back in Buffalo.

It felt strange—because, for some reason, there was a quiet sense of hope. A feeling that maybe—just maybe—my father could recover from at least some of what was afflicting him. He even began talking about the future again.

I don't know whether he did that to comfort those around him, or because he truly believed there was still a future ahead for him. Maybe it was both. For the time being, the doctors were treating him with the intention of healing him. And that alone changed the atmosphere.

I came to Buffalo for one simple reason: I had made a promise.

"I'll see you Friday."

And I keep my promises.

So there we were—my father and me—sitting together in a hospital room in Buffalo, New York. Once again, Janice had to go to Skateland, which meant I stayed behind to watch over him. But this visit was very different from the first.

This time, there were nurses. Doctors. Machines. Alarms. If anything went wrong, help would arrive within seconds. That knowledge alone allowed me to relax in a way I hadn't before.

Once the room grew quiet and it was just the two of us, my father turned to me and asked the question I hadn't expected—but somehow knew was coming.

"How is your mother?"

And just like that, the past came rushing back into the room.

My mother. The one person he talked about more than he talked about himself. When I was younger, it irritated the hell out of me. I didn't want commentary about my mother and her life from the man who had caused so much pain. But as an adult—after living enough life to understand how people break, how they heal, how they love poorly because they were taught poorly—I understood.

I'll tell you this: the person my father talked to me about more than anyone else—even more than he talked about himself—was my mother.

When I was younger, that bothered me. I didn't need to hear what my father thought about my mother. It felt inappropriate, intrusive, and unfair. But as I grew older and began to experience life as an adult, I started to understand why he talked about her so much.

As harsh as he could be—no matter how mean his words sometimes sounded—I always knew one thing to be true: my father loved my mother.

The tragedy is that he was never taught how to love.

He came from a hostile family environment, one rooted in rigidity, punishment, and emotional scarcity. And when he became an adult, he did nothing to change that approach to relationships. As a result, his warped understanding of love carried forward—passed down, unintentionally, to yet another generation.

My generation.

When he asked about my mother that day, I answered simply. *"She's doing quite well."*

I didn't offer details. After more than thirty years apart, I felt that the specifics of her life were no longer his to know. Some boundaries arrive late—but when they do, they matter.

Then he asked about my brother.

At that point, my brother and I didn't have much of a relationship. The only honest answer I could give was, *"He's fine. That's all I know."*

He asked if I talked to him.

"No," I said.

That was the end of the conversation.

Shortly afterward, the nurses came in to bathe my father and asked me to step out of the room. I complied and went downstairs to grab something to eat. But as I walked away, I couldn't shake the image of my father's face—the look of quiet regret that appeared when I told him about my mother, my brother, and the distance between us.

It wasn't dramatic.

It wasn't spoken.

But it was unmistakable.

As I sat there eating, memories of our time together as a family surfaced—fragmented. My earliest memories of our family center on a time of transition—when my sisters and I were still living together and my mother was pregnant with my brother. By the time my brother was born, to the best of my recollection, the only sister still living in the house was my sister Marina.

Marina was incredibly kind to me. She was a genuinely good big sister.

She took the time to play with me, and one of our favorite games was Batman and Robin. I was obsessed. I had all the big, eight-inch-tall action figures—Batman, Robin, the Joker, Catwoman, Batgirl, the Riddler, the Penguin—on and on. Those figures weren't just toys; they were entire worlds I could escape into.

One year—something that still stands out vividly—Adam West and Burt Ward came to the Armory on Michigan Street in Buffalo. They were there for a car show, and both of them were dressed as Batman and Robin. My mom and dad took me to see them, and to this day, it remains one of the most exciting memories of my childhood.

I remember standing in line, clutching a photo, waiting to get it autographed. *Man, I wish I had kept that photo.* When we finally reached the table, my father stood just behind us while my mother stood right next to me.

Adam West took the photo from my hands, signed it—and then looked up at my mother.

"Man," he said, *"what a gorgeous creature."*

In that instant, Adam West created a brand-new villain.

My father.

I am absolutely certain that my dad wanted to kick his ass without hesitation. No doubt about it.

All these years later, I still remember that moment like it happened yesterday.

A few years before Adam West passed away, he was in Indianapolis signing autographs. There was a billboard advertising the event. I remember calling my mom and saying, *"Hey—your boyfriend is in town."*

She just laughed.

And so did I.

It's funny how memory works. The moments that stay with us aren't always the heavy ones. Sometimes they're the lighthearted, absurd, almost cinematic scenes that remind us we were once just kids—standing in line, holding a photo, believing that Batman was real.

For a brief moment, our family was intact when my brother was born.

I remember family trips—real family trips—to places like Cape Cod and Cedar Point. Those were our regular destinations, the kind of trips families planned, packed for, and talked about afterward. For a while, life felt almost normal.

Around that same time, my father started promoting musical acts. One of them was a group called Sabata, and through that, we traveled around the country with them. One of the members—the keyboardist—was a young man named Curtis Williams. Curtis was incredibly talented, but more importantly, he was a genuinely good person.

He later went on to play keyboards for Kool & the Gang, and if my memory serves me right, he also became the keyboardist for The Tonight Show with Jay Leno. His father and my father were close friends, and Curtis was always kind to me—never talking down, never distant, just real.

The last time I saw him, years later, he had bought a house back in Buffalo and was married. He'd stop by my dad's place from time to time, and he always treated me with respect.

One day, I ran into him at Tops Friendly Markets—the store around the corner from our house. (Yes, this is the second time I've mentioned Tops. If anyone there is reading this and wants to sponsor my podcast, I'm open to negotiations.)

Some kids from high school saw me standing there, casually talking with Curtis. Overnight, I gained instant street credibility. For weeks afterward, kids at school talked about the level of *"juice"* I had. Apparently, proximity to celebrity mattered—even if it happened next to the deli counter.

We also lived next door to Reggie McKenzie, one of the most well-known offensive linemen for the Buffalo Bills at the time. He was very close friends with O. J. Simpson, who used to come by the house often. Whenever he saw me, he gave me the nickname *"Star."*

We all know what happened later in O.J.'s life. When everything unfolded with his ex-wife and his subsequent arrest, it genuinely broke my heart. Not because I excused anything—but because it shattered an image from childhood that had once felt untouchable.

My father also had many friends who were more business associates than anything else. Yet, interestingly, their wives all loved my mother. They helped her build the life she eventually came to live—upper-middle-class Buffalo, stable, grounded. And what says a lot about her is this: those women remained her friends long after she and my father separated for good.

I know now that many things in my parents' relationship were not right. But my mother worked hard to shield my brother and me from that reality. Whether it was because we were too young or because she was determined to protect us, she did an exceptional job of making sure we lived what appeared to be a normal life—just like everyone else in our neighborhood in East Amherst.

Looking back, that may have been one of her greatest gifts to us.

We didn't know everything.

We didn't see everything.

But for a time, we were allowed to just be kids—surrounded by music, road trips, famous neighbors, and a version of family that, however imperfect, felt real while it lasted.

One day, my mother could no longer shield us from the reality of what was happening inside our home.

My parents had an argument—no, a fight—and it exploded. Whatever line had been crossed that day, my mother decided it was time to leave. She was going back to Indiana.

I don't know what the fight was about. I still don't. What I *do* know is that I had just finished kindergarten and was getting ready to start first grade. I was still young enough to measure time by school years and summers, not by consequences.

Back then, whenever we made the long drive, Cedar Point was always a stop along the way. Years ago, there was also a SeaWorld Akron, and we'd stop there too before heading back to Buffalo. That place changed me.

That's where I fell in love with orcas.

I collected rubber orca toys—along with dolphins and sharks—and carried them everywhere. They were my comfort. My fascination only deepened when I saw the movie *Orca*. I remember my mom taking my sister Marina and me to see it. Even now, when it comes on television—which is rare—I think about that moment. I believe it was the very first movie I remember seeing in a theater.

Those toys matter to this story.

Because when my mom got my brother and me ready to leave, we weren't just packing—we were fleeing our own home.

I remember the urgency. The tension. The way everything felt rushed and wrong. As we were running out, I remember shouting, *"Mom—my fish!"* I was talking about my toys. My orcas. The things that made me feel safe.

I remember my dad saying something like, *"Fuck those fish."*

That's how I remember it. Whether those were his exact words or not, the meaning was clear: *don't worry about that.* And maybe my memory is shaped by years of context—but the feeling of dismissal was real.

We ran out of the house. I remember my dad running after us. My mom veered into the backyard, and somehow—we got away.

Suddenly, we were running through the backyards of Fox Hunt Farms—at the time, one of the most exclusive neighborhoods in all of Western New York. Famous hockey players. Football players. Musicians. Political leaders lived there.

And there we were.

A young mother.

Two young boys.

Running.

Even now, at fifty-four years old, I still don't fully understand *why* we were running. I just know that we were.

I remember my mom knocking on the back door of a stranger's house. They let us in. The woman fed us. I remember my mother standing at the window, watching my father drive past—again and again—clearly looking for us.

She was on the phone with her parents—my grandparents—making travel arrangements to get us back to Indiana.

That day marked the end of one life and the beginning of another.

I didn't understand it then. I barely understand it now. But I know this: childhood isn't always lost in a single moment. Sometimes it slips away while you're clutching rubber fish, running through manicured backyards, learning—far too early—that safety is something that can disappear without warning.

When night fell, the woman who had let us into her home took us to the airport in Buffalo. Not long after, we were on a plane headed to Indianapolis, Indiana.

I don't remember her name.

With all the years that have passed, she may no longer be with us. But I remember *what she did*. She showed extraordinary kindness to a frightened mother and two small boys. Buffalo is often called *the City of Good Neighbors*, and wherever that woman may be now, she embodied exactly what that phrase is supposed to mean—showing up for strangers in both good times and bad.

At six years old, I was suddenly exposed to a different side of life.

In truth, it was a life I had already been living—I just didn't know it yet. My mother had been incredibly strong, shielding me from realities she shouldn't have had to manage alone. As I said earlier in this book, she did everything she could to make sure my relationship with my father remained strong and healthy.

And even during that traumatic time—even now, as I write this and can still see that day clearly in my mind—I still loved my father.

As I've said before, my father came from an environment where love was deeply warped and poorly modeled. He never stopped to examine that reality or to understand that love does not look the way he had learned it. And because of that, he repeated patterns he never questioned.

We arrived in Indiana and settled in quickly. For the first time in my life, I was living away from my father.

I began school at Annunciation Catholic School in Brazil, Indiana. I remember my teacher, Sister Catherine. She was kind, firm, and loving. She didn't dress like a traditional nun—she had short gray hair—and she carried herself with calm authority. She made me feel safe.

I remember the kids I went to school with there. In fact, some of them are still my friends to this day. That alone tells you how formative that time was.

I remember having my seventh birthday party at Burger Chef. It was bought out by Hardee's about seven years later. It's funny—people from Brazil still mention Burger Chef on Facebook from time to time. I'm too young to remember what the hamburgers actually tasted like. Truthfully, they probably weren't much different from anyone else's.

I think what people really miss isn't the food.

They miss the time.

And while nostalgia can be comforting, I've learned something important over the years: some *old times* are not times we should ever try to recreate. Some moments are meant to be remembered, understood, and then left where they belong—so we can move forward without pretending they were better than they really were.

That lesson, like so many others in my life, arrived quietly—on a plane, in the dark, leaving one life behind and stepping into another I didn't yet understand.

Those few months away from my father were, in many ways, peaceful. I was young, and I don't think I fully understood the gravity of what had happened. At that age, peace doesn't come from understanding—it comes from routine. And I remember settling into life in Brazil, Indiana, fairly comfortably.

Toward the end of my first-grade year, my mother—who was attending school elsewhere in Indiana—was preparing to move there. I did *not* want to go. I had finally found my footing in Brazil. Looking back, it's strange to think that at seven years old I was already experiencing yet another transition—one I didn't fully understand, but deeply felt.

What I do remember clearly is longing for Buffalo.

I remember calling my father and telling him I wanted to come home.

And my father was glad to come get me.

When I look back on that moment now, I see it as a lesson with two very different interpretations.

The first is this: it was 1977. My father was never married to my mother. DNA testing wasn't what it is today. He was living a *Playboy* lifestyle. So why would a man in that position want to come pick up a soon-to-be second grader and take on the responsibility of raising him?

As a father now, I genuinely admire him for that. He showed up. He took responsibility.

But there's another possible interpretation.

As I said earlier in this chapter, my father always loved my mother. And maybe—just maybe—taking her seven-year-old son 534 miles back to Buffalo was also a way of pulling her back into his orbit. A way of saying, *we're still connected.*

It could have been one reason.

It could have been the other.

It could have been both.

What matters is this: my father came and got me. He brought me home.

One of the most important lessons I take from that moment is simple—always be there when your children call.

I've been married multiple times, and I can't honestly say I was always an outstanding husband. But I hope—deeply hope—that I was an outstanding father. I hope my children know that they can always call me.

In fact, as I was writing this very chapter, one of my kids called me.

They know my phone is always on.

They know my door is always open.

Ironically, I learned that from my father.

To the best of his ability—and as warped as it may sound—he really *was* always a phone call away for his kids. Could he have done better? Absolutely. Could I have done better? Without question. And I truly hope that in this area, at least, I did better than he did.

But the truth remains:

When his son called, he came.

And sometimes, that's the difference between abandonment and memory.

Which brings me back to my sister Marina.

One of the biggest reasons I wanted to return to Buffalo was because I got to be with my Batman buddy again—the one who always made time for me, the one who played with me, protected me, and made me feel like I mattered.

One of my fondest memories of Marina happened during her senior year of high school. She took me with her to school for the entire day. I still remember it clearly. You probably couldn't do that now—insurance alone would shut that down immediately—but back then, it was allowed. And to me, it was one of the greatest days of my life.

I remember sitting in one of her classes while she handed me a piece of paper so I could write *"notes,"* just like she was doing. I felt important. Grown. Included. I truly looked up to her.

So when I went back to Buffalo, I knew I'd get to stay with Marina again. And for the first couple of months, that was true. I spent as much time with her as I possibly could. She worked at Skateland, and she took care of me in ways that went far beyond responsibility—she did it with genuine love.

Then one day, everything changed.

My sister was invited to a concert. That same day happened to be the Vermilion Room picnic—the annual event for my father's nightclub. When Marina asked if she could go to the concert instead, my father lost his mind.

And just like that, he kicked her out of the house.

I was seven years old, standing there, watching my favorite person in the world walk out the door.

My father was a man obsessed with *principle*. He would say things like, *"After all I've done for you, you're supposed to do this for me."* He believed loyalty meant compliance. Obligation over relationship.

One of the hardest lessons I learned from my father—one I've seen play out countless times since—is that you can destroy a lot of relationships by clinging too tightly to principle.

Principle matters.

But practicality matters too.

There are a lot of people who stood so firmly on principle that, by Christmas Day, principle was the only thing left in the room. There are nursing homes filled with people whose only visitor they have is principle.

That day, Marina left.

And I went to the Vermilion Room picnic with my father.

I remember watching her drive away in her AMC Pacer—purple. I remember that color clearly. I watched her turn onto Paradise Road and disappear, while I stood there next to my father, suddenly alone.

If I had known the phrase at seven years old, I probably would've thought to myself:

Boy… am I fucked.

That moment wasn't just about my sister leaving. It was the beginning of understanding something far bigger—that love, when mixed with control, can become something unrecognizable. And that sometimes, the people we lose first are the ones who loved us the most.

Chapter 4

You and I

Once the chaos of the hospital room had settled—the cleaning, the nurses, my father being washed and made comfortable—I came back upstairs after grabbing something to eat in the cafeteria.

Dad was awake.

I reached for the remote, and he told me to find something we could watch together. So there I was, sitting on the edge of a hospital bed, scrolling through channels with one of those overly complicated hospital remotes. And let me say this as a public service announcement: hospitals should have *far* better television options. With all the money spent on healthcare, premium cable or streaming should be standard. A Saturday morning in a hospital room with bad TV is borderline cruel. Consider this my official marketing suggestion.

Anyway, as I flipped through channels trying to find *anything* watchable, my father looked at me and said, *"Just you and me again, kid."*

I looked at him and smiled.

Almost immediately, he began reminiscing about the time when it really *was* just the two of us—when we lived together on our own, and I was still a little boy. He said, *"Remember when we used to go out, and I'd dress you up in suits?"*

He smiled—one of the biggest smiles I'd seen on his face in a very long time. You could tell he genuinely cherished that time. It wasn't nostalgia for the sake of nostalgia; it was joy. Pure and uncomplicated.

When my sister left all those years ago, and it became just my dad and me, I'll admit—seven-year-old me was scared. I didn't know what that meant or how it would turn out. But looking back now, that period was probably one of the greatest times I ever spent with my father.

Just me and him.

If you're old enough, you might remember the TV show **Silver Spoons**. It starred **Ricky Schroder** as a young boy being raised by his wealthy father. The whole show revolved around a father-son relationship—adventures, misunderstandings, love, and growing up together. **Alfonso Ribeiro** even played Ricky's best friend.

It was a fun show. And even though it came out *after* my time alone with my father, whenever I watched it—and I watched it every single week—I couldn't help but think back to those days in the late '70s. Just me and my dad. Suits. Dinners. Moments that felt small at the time but grew larger with every passing year.

Sitting there in that hospital room, decades later, I realized something: life has a strange way of circling back. Different setting. Different circumstances. Same bond.

Just you and me again, kid.

And this time, I understood exactly what that meant.

When my sister left that day—the one I talked about in the previous chapter—my father and I went straight to his nightclub picnic. It was held at Ellicott Creek Park, and I remember it like it happened yesterday.

Here I was, a seven-year-old boy, hanging out with the regulars from my father's bar.

And honestly? It didn't bother me at all.

I had fun.

The women at that picnic were especially attentive to me. Looking back now, I understand why. They weren't just being kind to a kid—they were auditioning. It was a subtle performance of *Look how good I am with your child*. A way of saying, *I could fit into your life. I could live in your very big house.*

My father was hip to all of that.

After the picnic, we went back home. School was starting soon, and my father needed to buy everything—school supplies, clothes, shoes, you name it. That was not something my father ever did alone. So, naturally, he invited a woman to come along with us.

Her name was Nora.

I remember her fondly. If you've ever seen WKRP in Cincinnati and remember the character Bailey, that's exactly what Nora looked like. She had that same gentle energy— soft-spoken, kind, thoughtful. She was very fond of my father, and I believe my father was fond of her too.

Sometimes we'd go to her house. She would cook us dinner. I'd watch television or mess around on her guitar— badly. After a while, my father and I would go back home, and that would be that.

There *was* a special relationship between my father and Nora.

But it was secret.

And in my father's eyes, it was taboo.

Nora was a white woman. My father was deeply afraid that being in a serious relationship with a white woman would create problems—real problems. He believed society would never allow it to be simple. That fear stayed with him for years.

In fact, much later in life, when I dated a white woman myself, my father warned me to be very careful. He talked to me at length about the pitfalls—not between me and the woman, but between us and the world. I brushed it off at the time, like most young men do.

But deep down, I understood.

The reason a serious relationship between my father and Nora never fully materialized wasn't a lack of connection—it was fear of society itself.

In the 1970s, mixed-race couples were not common. The first time I ever remember seeing a truly interracial couple was on the television sitcom The Jeffersons. And even then, many of the episodes that focused on that couple highlighted the challenges they faced.

Times have changed since then.

But not completely.

There are still challenges when it comes to mixed relationships—and this will not be the last time this subject comes up in this book. It threads through my father's life in ways that shaped his choices more than he ever admitted.

Because my father never pursued a serious relationship with Nora—and because relationships in general were unstable—he relied on many different people to help take care of me. Friends. Girlfriends. Bar regulars. Community members.

I learned early that love doesn't always come from one place.

Sometimes it comes in pieces.

Before getting into what came next, I have to say this: that period of my life was also when my father was fully living what I can only describe as a *Hugh Hefner lifestyle.*

There were people at my father's house *all the time*—many of them people I didn't even know. To be clear, everyone was kind to me, and nothing inappropriate ever happened. Still, looking back now, I can't help but wonder what the neighbors thought was going on inside that house.

There were scores of women around—sometimes it felt like dozens. A few guys would show up here and there to drink and hang out with my father, but for the most part, it was women. Everywhere.

At the same time, my father was remodeling the house. It was constantly being painted. New landscaping was going in. There were fountains outside—ornamental, dramatic, and very *extra*. My father thought it was all incredibly cool. As I grew older, I realized it was… kind of tacky.

But that was the vibe.

My father was living the playboy life—and his seven-year-old sidekick was right there with him.

I used to joke with my dad that I had *many, many stepmothers*. I'm not exaggerating when I say I might have had two or three stepmothers in a single day. Usually, the last "*stepmother*" who cooked dinner at night was the same one who made me breakfast in the morning and got me off to school.

What I found especially odd as I got older was realizing that during this time, my father had installed a mirror over his king-size bed. When I was a kid, I thought it was pretty cool. As an adult, I had a very different reaction:

Damn. My dad was kind of a freaky guy.

And yet—here's the part that still surprises people— through all the parties, the women, the noise, and the chaos, my father never ran from the responsibility of raising me. He didn't disappear. He didn't delegate me away.

Mondays were *our* day.

Every Monday, it was just me and him. I'd come home from school, and we'd go to the mall. I got an allowance every week—$15. In 1977, that was a *lot* of money. We'd hit the toy store, or we'd go to Woolworths.

And if we went to Woolworths, there was a 100% guarantee we were eating at the diner.

I absolutely loved Woolworth's hamburgers and fries. Loved them. And I always knew—if we were there—my dad was in the mood for one too.

Those Mondays mattered.

They were the calm inside the storm.

The routine inside the chaos.

And looking back now, I can see the contradiction clearly: my father's life was loud, excessive, and messy—but when it came to me, he showed up. Not perfectly. Not traditionally. But consistently.

And sometimes, consistency is the thing that sticks the longest.

It was during this time that I fell completely in love with Matchbox cars. I bought them every single week—dozens of them. That obsession quickly expanded to Star Wars action figures. My bedroom became a toy lover's paradise.

I had the *best* toys in the neighborhood.

My friends loved coming over because my house was basically a showroom. I had X-Wing fighters, the Millennium Falcon, TIE fighters—you name it, I had it. I also started collecting die-cast airplanes. Whenever my father traveled for business—or sent me to visit my mother—I'd come back with a plane.

Back then, airlines gave those planes away for free. Now you have to buy them in airport gift shops or coffee stands. Funny how that works.

What's even funnier is that now I have grandsons, and I carry on the tradition. I always buy them airplanes. They *love* them. In fact, the first thing they ask me when they see me is, *"Do you have an airplane?"*

I always make sure I do.

I try not to give them the same airline twice—though I'll admit, since I'm a rewards member with one airline, some of those planes are Amazon-bought and not airline-issued. They'll never know the difference… at least not until they're old enough to read this book.

Around this same time, my father also began grooming me—intentionally or not—to understand business. He took me to meetings. Real meetings. Banks. Executives. Celebrities. That's why he dressed me up in suits.

When he asked me in the hospital room years later, *"Remember when I used to dress you up in suits?"*—that's what he meant.

Those suits served two purposes.

The first was business.

The second was dining.

My father didn't love Woolworths as much as I did. He preferred a restaurant called The Cloister—one of the most elegant restaurants in all of Western New York. The Cloister was housed in one of Mark Twain's former homes, and everything about it was top-of-the-line.

I remember going there at seven years old and ordering lobster.

An entire lobster tail.

At seven.

To this day, lobster is still my favorite food. No matter where I am, if it's on the menu, that's what I order. In fact, in March of 2025, I was in Sydney, Australia, having dinner with my dear friend Dr. Angela Bennett, and I ate the best lobster I've ever had in my life.

Since then, it's been hard to find one that compares.

Looking back, I realize something important: my father taught me about abundance early—sometimes responsibly, sometimes excessively—but always memorably. Toys. Travel. Business. Food. Experiences.

Some lessons were deliberate.

Some were accidental.

But all of them stuck.

And now, when I hand my grandsons a little airplane and watch their faces light up, I realize how much of that joy— however imperfect its origins—was passed down.

My dad also did a lot of business with Rick James—the legendary artist most people immediately associate with *Super Freak*. But as iconic as that song is, Rick James made music that went far beyond it. My personal favorite has always been *You and I*.

Whenever my father would go to Rick's home in Orchard Park, I would tag along. Rick had an indoor swimming pool, and there I was—just a kid—nonchalantly swimming in the home of one of the biggest stars of that era, as if it were the most normal thing in the world.

I met quite a few people at Rick's house, but one of the most memorable was Teena Marie. At the time, she was young and just starting out. She was incredibly kind and even watched me a few times while I swam. I had no idea then how famous she would become. Looking back now, it feels surreal.

To this day, I still listen to both Rick James and Teena Marie. There will never be musicians quite like them again. They were raw, fearless, and extraordinarily talented—products of a musical era that simply doesn't exist anymore.

During all of this, my father was still running multiple businesses. He had the nightclub, which opened Wednesday through Sunday nights. He also had the skating rink, which ran Friday through Sunday. On school nights, my father would drop me off at my Aunt Sarah's house in East Amherst—just a short distance from where we lived.

I'd spend the night there, and she would take me to school in the morning.

The best part of staying there was spending time with my cousin Krissy. She was only a few months older than me, and honestly, she was more like a sister than a cousin. We had countless adventures together as kids—and yes, we got each other into a fair amount of trouble. Even as adults, we remained extremely close.

In 2019, Krissy lost her battle with cancer.

I remember driving from Indianapolis to Buffalo to see her one last time. I remember leaving that visit overwhelmed by how sweet and kind she had always been. She had wonderful children—children who have grown into successful, grounded men and women. I know that if Krissy were still here, she would be incredibly proud of them.

Watching them now, I know I am.

I don't see them as often as I should. I should be more present. Life gets in the way—but that's not an excuse. And if they happen to read this book before I get the chance to tell them myself, I want them to know this:

I am extremely proud of the men and women you have become.

Some relationships in life fade quietly.

Others leave marks that time can't erase.

Krissy was one of those people.

And even now, decades after swimming in celebrity pools and growing up far too fast, it's the love—quiet, loyal, and enduring—that matters most.

Most weeks followed a predictable rhythm.

I would stay at my Aunt Sarah's house on Wednesday and Thursday nights. On Friday night, my father would take me to the skating rink. After the final session, I'd sleep downstairs in the office while my dad was upstairs at the nightclub.

Saturday was more of the same. My father and I would go back to the rink, and I'd skate both sessions. When skating was over, I'd head back down to the office and wait for my father to wake me so we could go home together.

Sunday was a little different.

I would skate on Sunday too, but after the session ended, my Aunt Sarah would pick me up and take me back to her house. I'd stay there Sunday night and go to school on Monday, with Sarah dropping me off. Then Monday afternoon, I'd go home—and that was our time.

Just Dad and me.

One memory from the skating rink still stands out vividly. I was asleep in the office when a young Chaka Khan—who had been performing upstairs at my dad's nightclub—came downstairs to wake me up. That moment is burned into my memory. Even now, I still listen to her music and love it just as much.

The nightclub—The Vermilion Room—drew some of the biggest names in music during the 1970s. It was *the* nightclub in Western New York. I've mentioned Chaka Khan, but there were so many others: Teddy Pendergrass, Stevie Wonder, Earth, Wind & Fire—you name it. If you were a major R&B or funk act in the '70s, chances are you passed through the Vermilion Room.

As a kid, it felt incredible. Surreal. Like living inside a backstage pass.

At some point, though, I realized something else.

I just wanted to be with my father.

For reasons I didn't fully understand at the time, I no longer wanted to stay at Aunt Sarah's. I wanted to be where my dad was. So I stayed at the skating rink every night—sleeping in the office, going to school, doing everything I was supposed to do.

Here I am now, in my mid-fifties, and I still have strange sleep patterns. I honestly believe they started back then—falling asleep on couches and office floors, waking up at odd hours, always half-aware, always waiting.

It's funny what stays with us.

Some kids grow up with bedtime stories and nightlights. I grew up with rink lights, nightclub music echoing through walls, and the hum of a life that never really shut off.

And somehow, in the middle of all that noise, all I really wanted was my dad nearby.

Once it was just my father and me—completely—he had to find people to help take care of me.

Many of those people were women from the nightclub. Some of them, my father later told me, were strippers. What matters to me now isn't the label—it's what they did.

They were kind to me.

They played Matchbox cars with me. They played Star Wars with me. They fed me. They made sure I was ready for school. When I got sick, they took care of me. They showed patience, gentleness, and responsibility at a time when my life was anything but stable.

That period of my childhood was deeply impressionable. It shaped how I see people to this day.

People in the sex industry are looked down on relentlessly. I never have. And the reason is simple: many people don't end up there by choice—they end up there by necessity. Life corners them. Circumstances narrow. Options disappear.

That understanding stayed with me.

Recently, I released a book called Stories of Transgression and Recovery. It became a bestseller. The book explores how people fall into addiction, how they survive it, and how they find their way out. The contributors—especially the women— are some of the bravest people I've ever met.

When I shared the book on social media, someone left a cruel comment. Clearly referencing my brother's book Can't Hurt Me, they wrote something like:

"Another Trunnis hanging out and promoting strippers and hookers again."

Now, I understand social media. The moment you post anything, you invite opinions. Some people will like what you say. Some will hate it. Thick skin is mandatory.

But that comment hit deeper than most.

Immediately, two things came to mind.

First, the courage of the women who shared their stories in this book—who laid their lives bare so others might feel less alone.

Second, the women from my childhood—the ones society loves to judge—who cared for me when I was seven years old.

So I replied:

"You can save a lot of money if you stop thinking about hookers, don't buy my book, and go fuck yourself."

One of the authors from Stories of Transgression and Recovery saw the exchange and said to me, *"That's what we face all the time."*

Here she was—a reformed alcoholic and former sex worker—doing the hardest work of her life, and still being reduced to ignorance by strangers.

Here's the truth most people refuse to confront:

Any one of us could have ended up there if one small circumstance in our lives had changed.

That idea isn't new. Sting captured it perfectly in his song Tomorrow We'll See, which tells the story of a male prostitute. It's a heartbreaking song. One line in particular has always stayed with me:

"Don't judge me—you could be me in another life, in another set of circumstances."

That line is absolutely true.

Because of what I experienced at seven years old, I learned early to judge people by the content of their character—not their résumé, not their past, not their worst chapter.

Today, my friends range from PhDs to reformed drug addicts, and everything in between. I don't care where you came from. I don't care what you did to survive.

But I care deeply about who you are inside—your integrity, your compassion, and your willingness to grow.

That lesson didn't come from a classroom.

It came from a childhood where the people society looks down on were the very ones who showed me what humanity actually looks like.

Anyway, back to the story.

As I mentioned earlier, by this time, I was flying back to Indiana once a month to see my mother. She was living in Terre Haute and going to school. I'd fly in for a weekend, spend time with her, and then return to Buffalo.

One of those weekends was just before Thanksgiving in 1978.

Like most weekends with my mom, it was fun. I remember going to the airport with my mother and my grandmother. Back then—long before 9/11—you could walk all the way to the gate with the passenger. I remember them escorting me right up to the front.

The airline was Allegheny Airlines.

I remember sitting by the window—my favorite seat then and still my favorite seat now. I remember looking out as the plane prepared to taxi and seeing my mother standing there. She was crying, watching her young son leave again. My grandmother stood beside her, waving, one hand on my mother's shoulder. I waved back as hard as I could.

That image stayed with me.

I flew back to Buffalo and was picked up by someone who worked at Skateland. When we arrived, my father was standing at the front door, waiting for me like he always did. We went home that night.

The next morning, as I was getting ready for school, the weight of leaving my mother hit me harder than it ever had before. Something about that trip felt different. Heavy. Real.

And while I was tying my shoes, I asked my father a question that came straight from my seven-year-old heart:

"Dad... do you love my mom?"

He didn't hesitate.

"Yes," he said. *"I do love your mother."*

I went to school that day. When I came home, there was another woman there—someone new—to take care of me. And for the first time, I *knew* something was wrong.

Without thinking—and right in front of her—I said, *"Dad, I thought you loved my mom."*

The room went silent.

Here I was, seven years old, standing toe-to-toe with the toughest man I had ever known, challenging him in front of his date. Looking back, I think my father understood that I didn't yet grasp the complexities of adult relationships. I didn't get in trouble. He simply told me to go upstairs and get ready for bed.

The next morning, something felt different.

I expected the woman to wake me up and get me ready for school—but it was my dad. He woke me up, helped me get dressed, and walked me through the morning routine himself.

Before I got on the bus, he said, *"After Skateland closes on Sunday, you and I are flying to Indiana together."*

That day at school was one of the happiest days I can remember.

True to his word, we flew to Indiana, rented a car, and drove to Terre Haute. We went to my mother's apartment. And for the first time in almost two years, all of us stood in the same room together.

It was cordial.

Warm.

Almost hopeful.

That Wednesday morning, my dad and I flew back to Buffalo. I didn't know when I'd see my mother again. I assumed maybe Christmas—if I was lucky.

But then, the following Monday afternoon, after school, my father surprised me with a trip to the airport. At Buffalo Niagara International Airport, we picked up my mother and my brother.

My mom said she was staying until Christmas.

That Christmas, my grandfather—my dad's father—was there. All my sisters came. My soon-to-be brother-in-law David was there. My nephew Darnell too. It was the only Christmas where *everyone* was together.

I don't remember the presents. I don't even remember the meal. It was probably a traditional Christmas dinner.

What I remember is the feeling.

That Christmas was special.

Later in this book, you'll learn that holidays were rarely — if ever — celebrated in the Goggins family. But this one was different. This one mattered.

Christmas ended. School started again. And I began wondering when my mother would go back to Indiana.

Then one morning, something happened that changed everything.

It was my mother — not my father — who walked me to the bus stop.

She wasn't going back.

She was staying with us in Buffalo.

And at seven years old, standing there with my backpack on, I didn't have the language for it — but I knew I was witnessing something rare:

A family, however fragile, choosing to try again.

The year 1979 began in a way that felt almost sacred to me.

We were a family again.

In January of that year, my sister Marina got married, and for once, everyone was together — siblings, parents, extended family, all in the same place. I remember watching my father that day. He had a different smile on his face. Not the confident, performative smile he wore so often—but a softer one. A genuine one.

I smiled too.

My mother was back home. My brother was there. The house felt full—not just with people, but with possibility. For the first time in a long while, things felt balanced. Steady.

At seven years old, I didn't analyze it. I didn't question it. I didn't wait for the other shoe to drop.

To me, everything was exactly the way it was supposed to be.

And sometimes, even when life is fragile, those moments still matter. They become anchors—proof that, however briefly, things *did* come together.

Chapter 5

One Big Happy Family

Now with my computer closed and my father fully awake, Dad was in the mood for conversation. One conversation that he always had with me since my mother left in 1983 was about my mom. I could tell by the look on my dad's face what he was about to talk about. *"How is your mother?"* my father asked me. He went on to say, *"I have a good mind to have you call her. I would love to talk to her right now."* Though this may have been one of my father's dying wishes, I knew better than to dial my mother's number and have my father on the other end of that call. My mom was not in the same place my dad was, and for valid reason.

Now here I am, a 42-year-old man, and I understand that some things are better left alone. A lot of people who read my brother's book, and know me or my mother, go to my mother and ask why she went back; some even ask why she stayed. They ask that question with a sense of amazement that my mother was willing to take what she took for so long. As a parent, I am now able to answer this based on my own experiences in life. I am quite certain my mother stayed or even came back because she wanted her boys to be together. She was brought up in a family that stayed together, and ironically, my father was also brought up in a family that stayed together.

When it comes to being a parent, principle and practicality sometimes go out the window. The mission of preservation becomes first and foremost. Preservation of a parent-child relationship and preservation of sibling relationships take precedence over principle and practicality. We see in the animal kingdom that sacrifice is one of the ultimate weapons in protecting the young. Many parents will agree with that explanation because they have experienced it and done it for their children. In addition, there are those who may disagree with that explanation. I can only surmise that those who disagree have either never had children or should not be parents at all.

Again, my father started reminiscing about the times he had with my mother. *"Boy, we had some good times, me and your mother."* And as a child, I witnessed those good times. There truly were good times.

When my mother first came back from Indiana, there were indeed some fun times. Almost instantaneously, my father started buying my mother lavish gifts. I remember shortly after my mother came back, my dad traded in his Cadillac Sedan DeVille for a 1977 Cadillac Eldorado. I absolutely loved that car. What I loved most about it was the built-in CB radio, which for you young folks was the equivalent of having a cell phone now.

Plus, my favorite movie at the time was *Smokey and the Bandit*, and that movie made CBs more popular than ever. One thing I remember vividly about that Eldorado was when my father was getting ready to buy another car and called his father—my grandfather—to the house. My grandfather came over and was talking to me and my brother David while my father was running back and forth getting things done with the Eldorado. My grandfather was none the wiser. When my father finished, he walked in the room with a set of Cadillac keys and handed them to my grandfather.

My grandfather was not a wealthy man; in fact, I do not believe he had any formal education past elementary school. Remember, he was born in Anniston, Alabama, in 1902, and that surely was not a good time for Black people. Education was not considered important. My grandfather raised a very large family and worked extremely hard, but he was never in a position to own a Cadillac. The look of joy on his face when he received those keys is something I will never forget.

I would tell you that he cried, but his last name is Goggins. I do remember my grandfather looking at David and me, saying that my father was a good son and that when we reached a certain age, we needed to treat our parents the same way. I truly believe those words stuck with David and me later in life. My father then bought a 1979 Cadillac Seville, and I remember the look on my mother's face when we got it—she absolutely loved it. However, looks can be deceiving.

I'd like to be the first to tell you that that car was the ultimate piece of shit. As a matter of fact, if you ever look in Webster's Dictionary under the word lemon, you'd see a picture of a blue 1979 Cadillac Seville. My father and mother had more trouble with that car than with any other car they ever owned. And the funny thing is, he bought it brand new. I remember my father returning to the dealership repeatedly to complain.

One time, we were going to the grocery store and were at the corner of Maple and Transit—one of the busiest intersections in Western New York—when the car stalled making a left turn, dead in the middle of the intersection. Pretty soon, my father had had enough and decided it was time to get rid of that car and stop supporting Cadillac. He traded it in and literally paid cash for a 1980 Mercedes 450 SLC. At the time, that was one of the premier cars on the road, and it was extremely rare.

I remember my mother being absolutely excited about that car. In addition to cars, my mother also got top-of-the-line fur coats, jewelry—you name it. My dad was literally on a mission to buy my mother's affection. Things were also pretty good for David and me during this time. I remember being able to play Little League football for the Williamsville Sweet Home Football League.

You wouldn't know it by looking at me now—at 5'7" and 175 pounds—but I was one of the bigger kids in elementary school. I played defensive tackle. I attributed that to my porky build and wore number 74. That team went all the way to the championship and lost to a team called Air Force, which had one player who was unstoppable. I still remember his name: Jimmy Verna. I never saw that kid again, but I will never forget his talent in fourth-grade football.

Also during that time, my parents actually hired a nanny. Her name was Mrs. Haywood, and she was one of the sweetest women I ever knew. She watched us as my mother and father went to Skateland and the Vermillion Room. During this time, the Vermillion Room was growing in reputation. My mother played a key role during that growth.

In front of my desk to this day, I still have a newspaper article—mounted—that features my mother, father, and uncle. It was in the Courier Express, a now-defunct Buffalo newspaper, talking about one of the nights they hosted called Western Night. Also during this time, my dad decided to totally remodel the skating rink. At the time, his design was state-of-the-art. It had two rinks: one for kids and one for experienced skaters.

In addition to the success at the nightclub and skating rink, Dad was finding new success in other ventures. My parents went on important trips with Rick James, and he was constantly doing music promotions with Eddie O'Jay. For those of you who are music buffs, yes, that is who the famous group The O'Jays are named after. As far as family was concerned, we were becoming the semblance of what a family should look like. My father would have summer trips where he'd invite and pay for my sisters and their families to go to Thousand Islands and Martha's Vineyard.

Those were fantastic trips. I also remember my father welcoming and inviting my mother's parents on trips. I absolutely loved when my mother's parents came to town. My father would buy Gucci handbags and fur coats not only for my mother but for her mother as well. I truly believe that when my father said, *"Man, your mother had fun,"* he was referring to the period between 1978 and 1981.

Yes indeed, it was a fun time. It was also a time when I was becoming an adolescent. I was becoming more aware of things around me. My interpretation was no longer influenced solely by what my parents wanted me to believe but by what I began to observe on my own. I remember during this time becoming aware of the word *"recession"*.

I remember watching the news and hearing about how bad the economy was in the early '80s. That bad economy had a profound effect on Skateland and the Vermillion Room. My father could no longer afford a nanny, so we started going to Skateland all the time. Gone were the fancy restaurants; instead, my mother prepared food at home and took it to Skateland to cook on a hot plate right on the office floor. I am not saying this for sympathy—small businesses go through hard times, and we were no exception.

It was also during this time that I began working behind the concession stand at Skateland, not just two or three hours but 20 to 35 hours a week. I was 10 years old when I started working long hours. In addition to those hours, I was required, with no exceptions, to maintain good grades. I remember my last day of fourth grade. My teacher was Mr. Graham, one of my favorite teachers of all time, and we still communicate today. I remember going home from the last day of fourth grade and passing out.

My mother was concerned and took me to the emergency room, where I was diagnosed with chronic fatigue. Here I was, a 10-year-old kid suffering from chronic fatigue. I often wonder if that diagnosis—had it occurred 20 years later— would have led to much more serious consequences for my parents. Clearly, my father's decision to make sure I worked long hours had a negative effect on me.

I am not saying that kids should not learn the value of work; I am saying that the value should be balanced with a child being a child and being able to handle what a 10-year-old can handle. No child should work the hours I worked growing up. As I mentioned earlier, I was becoming more aware of things around me. That awareness was due to age and maturity. One thing I was not aware of was what was actually happening beneath the surface of what I thought was a pretty cool family.

I know that in the book Can't Hurt Me, my brother talked about abuse. I'm going to be very honest: all the friends I knew got their ass whipped too, so at the time I never considered that I was being abused. The only thing I thought was that my dad was stronger than the rest of the dads, so my ass-whoopings were more extreme. As I grew up, I realized that clearly the way my brother and I were treated went beyond the pale of natural discipline. What I also wasn't aware of was that my father was literally sabotaging his family.

All the women I mentioned earlier in the chapter, from when Dad and I lived together, never really went anywhere; they just sat in the shadows—at least that's what my dad thought. My father was still messing around with other women, and my mother knew about it and did a fantastic job of keeping it away from David and me. My mother told me that Rick James really did like her and hated the fact that my dad was doing that to her. He actually found subtle ways to embarrass my father and call him out. She shared a couple of those stories with me.

The relationship between my father and Rick James was probably the weirdest relationship in the world. But what also gets me is this: with all the stories about Rick James out there—including him serving prison time—the fact that he had the moral fortitude to call out my father's indiscretions is extremely ironic. With all the things my mom did to cover and preserve my brother's and my perception of our father, she could not keep it covered forever. In 1982, my father had a heart attack. I still remember the day we had to call an ambulance to the house.

It was the efforts of my mother that kept my father alive that day. However, that day also proved terminal to our family. Little did we know, my father's medical episode would prove fatal, not to him, but to his family.

Chapter 6

1983 — The Year That Changed Everything

As I sat there listening to my father reminisce about the *"good times"* he and my mother once shared, I watched his face begin to change. It was subtle at first—a tightening around the eyes, a slight shift in posture—but then even the tone of his voice softened and grew heavier. He paused mid-thought and went silent. For a brief moment, he looked away from me, as if staring into a place only he could see. Then he turned back and said quietly, almost like a confession, *"Tell your mother I'm sorry. I didn't do that right."*

I didn't hesitate. I looked him directly in the eyes and replied, *"No—you didn't do that right."*

We both knew exactly what he was referring to.

Whenever my mind drifts back to that period of my life, I simply label it *1983*. That year stands alone. It was, without question, one of the worst years I have ever lived through—and for a long time, I believed it *was* the worst year of my life. It was a year defined by violence, uncertainty, and trauma. Even now, I can say with clarity that what happened during that single year shaped my relationship with every family member I've ever had. It didn't just affect us in the moment — it set the tone for decades. It laid the groundwork for many of the relationship struggles I would carry into adulthood.

For years, I convinced myself that I didn't need to talk to anyone about that time. I told myself I was fine. That I had moved on. That I was strong enough to handle it alone.

I was wrong.

What most people don't realize is that 1983 didn't truly begin in January of that year — it started in early 1982, while my father was lying in a hospital bed recovering from a heart episode. It was during that time that I first learned about Janice. Our initial introduction was anything but good. I had seen her around the building before, often working there, but I didn't know who she really was or what role she would come to play in my life.

Years later, my father told me that when my mother returned to Buffalo in 1978, he had been blunt with her — that he had told her outright that Janice existed. But once you understand the full context, once you trace the events from the moment my father left that hospital bed in 1982 to the day my mother finally walked away in August of 1983, that claim becomes hard to believe. The evidence simply doesn't support the simplicity of his statement.

Now, as a grown man—one not much older than my father was when all of this unfolded—I can look back and recognize what was really happening. The world he was trying to build, trying desperately to hold together—with my mother on one side and Janice on the other—was collapsing in on him. And when that world began to crumble, his reactions toward his family revealed everything. Confusion turned into distance. Guilt turned into defensiveness. And love, fractured by secrecy and fear, became something unrecognizable.

That moment—him asking me to tell my mother he was sorry—was not just an apology. It was an admission. One that came too late to change the past, but not too late to name it for what it truly was.

When I first met Janice, I was working in the ticket booth at Skateland. I was eleven years old. At that age, Skateland wasn't just my home—it was my entire world. Like most kids my age, I had developed a sense of humor with the employees. It was lighthearted, casual, and, in my mind, harmless.

I remember Janice needing access to the office. My mother was already inside. As she approached, I jokingly—at least I thought it was joking—said, *"What do you want?"* I didn't pause to think. I didn't assign any meaning to it. To me, it was nothing more than a kid being a kid.

Not long after that, I found myself at the hospital visiting my father. That's when everything shifted. My father demanded that I go back and apologize to Janice for the way I had treated her. To this day, I don't fully remember what I was supposedly in trouble for—but I vividly remember crying as I apologized. Not because I felt guilty. Not because I thought I had done something wrong. I cried because I genuinely believed I hadn't. I was confused, embarrassed, and powerless.

That moment set the stage—at least for me.

When my father was released from the hospital, it felt like a veil had been lifted, revealing a division that could no longer be hidden. A new split took shape inside Skateland itself. My mother—who once stood beside my father in the Vermilion Room, equal and present—was now relegated to Skateland only. She was no longer allowed upstairs. Janice, on the other hand, was confined to the Vermilion Room and not permitted to come downstairs, at least temporarily. The building had been physically divided, just like the family.

Around that same time, Reaganomics was beginning to take hold, and business started improving again. Money was flowing back in. But did that mean relief for us kids? Did it mean fewer hours, less pressure, or more freedom?

Not even close.

Instead, it meant I had to work harder. And worse, my eight-year-old brother was now expected to work too.

I will never forget watching him at that age—eight years old—working the skate room. Long hours. Real responsibility. He had to keep rented roller skates perfectly organized, maintain order, and move with urgency, all while knowing that any mistake could bring down the full weight of my father's wrath. Failure was not an option.

Sometimes I look at eight-year-olds today—kids who struggle to tie their shoes or stay focused for ten minutes—and I'm struck by the contrast. My brother wasn't just a child trying to grow up; he was a child forced to perform like an adult. That wasn't character-building. That was survival.

Those moments weren't isolated incidents. They were signals. Warnings. Early lessons about power, loyalty, and control. And whether I understood it then or not, the world I knew was already fracturing—one apology, one rule, and one silent boundary at a time.

Yet even in the middle of all that turmoil—amid the chaos at home and the hard, grinding child labor that David and I endured—there was a bright spot. Her name was Lisa McNeil.

Lisa was a little older than us, but in every way that mattered, she became a big sister. She showed up to Skateland every single time it was open, without fail. Rain or shine, good days or bad ones, Lisa was there. And when the skating sessions ended—when most people were eager to leave—she stayed behind. She helped us clean. She helped us reset. She helped us breathe.

You've already heard some of the stories in my brother's book about what we had to do after the sessions were over— the exhaustion, the endless tasks, the feeling that the work never truly ended. But Lisa was there in those moments. She didn't have to be. No one asked her to be. She simply chose to help carry our cross.

At an age when many people are focused only on themselves, Lisa noticed two kids who were struggling and stepped into their lives with kindness, consistency, and quiet strength. She made things lighter—not by changing our circumstances, but by standing beside us in them.

All these years later, I'm still in contact with her, and I still see her as a big sister. She will probably never fully understand what those moments meant to me, or how much her presence mattered during a time when so much felt unstable and unfair. But her impact never faded.

Lisa eventually joined the Navy and now lives in Texas. And it doesn't surprise me at all that she continues to help people. Some people are just wired that way—they show up, they serve, and they leave places better than they found them.

It's always beautiful to be reminded that people like that exist in this world. Especially when you needed one most—and didn't even know how to ask.

By 1982 and 1983, family trips had stopped entirely. In fact, *family time* as I knew it disappeared altogether. As a child, I believed that was a punishment—and in many ways, it was. But as a man, with the benefit of distance and clarity, I understand that those moments also vanished because my father was under immense pressure to divide himself between two women. That pressure didn't excuse what happened, nor does it earn my sympathy—but it does explain the source. It was pressure he created himself, and it spilled over onto everyone around him.

Instead of being absorbed or resolved, that pressure was released downward—onto David and me.

I remember being in sixth grade at Mill Middle School during that time. Middle school alone is difficult enough: new social hierarchies, new expectations, new insecurities. But layered on top of that were long hours of hard work at Skateland and an unrelenting demand for perfection. Good grades were not encouraged; they were *required*. There was no margin for error, no room for adjustment, no allowance for being a kid.

I still remember bringing home my very first sixth-grade report card. It was the worst one I ever had. My cumulative average was a 67.3 percent. That number is burned into my memory.

My brother has written openly about abuse in his book, and I've often tried to steer away from revisiting those details. There's no value in beating a dead horse—it happened, it was horrible, and I've had to move on. But this moment stands apart. This was the worst beating I ever received.

I don't remember many whippings from my father, but I remember this one vividly. I remember some of the words he said. I remember the sound of his voice. I remember the physical pain afterward. Even as I write this now, I can still see it—looking at my back, the sides of my legs, and noticing enormous bruises everywhere. The pain didn't fade quickly; it lingered, both physically and emotionally.

If I'm forced to find one sliver of good in that moment—and I truly have to work hard to do so—it's this: that beating forged an unusually high tolerance for pain in me. That may sound strange, but it's true. Over the years, when I've played sports or pushed my body past its limits, people have asked how I keep going through broken fingers, pulled muscles, or injuries that would stop others. I usually joke and say, *"I'm just tough—I don't feel pain."*

That's not true.

I feel pain. I always have. But 1983 taught me how to *play through it*. How to get up when everything in you says stay down. How to keep walking when stopping feels safer. That ability—distorted as its origin may be—has carried me through many difficult seasons of life. That so-called *"life skill"* was forged during this time.

What I also remember vividly is the isolation. The quiet. The sense that I was alone inside my own world, carrying burdens no child should have to shoulder. There was no family togetherness to retreat into, no safe emotional harbor. Just responsibility, expectation, and silence.

Those years didn't just hurt—they shaped me. And while I've spent much of my life unlearning the damage they caused, I can't deny that the endurance I rely on today was born in that crucible.

My grandfather, Douglas Goggins, used to pick David and me up for church every Saturday night. It was something we genuinely looked forward to. Those evenings felt safe. Predictable. They gave us a sense of belonging that we didn't even realize we needed as much as we did. Before 1982, my mother's cousin Sammy worked the concession stand on Saturday nights, which meant we could spend time with our grandfather while still being close to family. Those nights were small gifts of normalcy in an otherwise demanding world.

Then, suddenly, those Saturday nights ended.

Just like that, we were cut off—not only from our grandfather but also from my mother's parents altogether. At the time, I didn't fully understand what was happening. I just knew something important had been taken away. As I've grown older, I've come to understand that isolation is one of the most powerful tools an abuser can use. The more isolated someone becomes, the easier it is to control them. The fewer outside voices there are, the fewer witnesses, the fewer places of refuge. And for a while, that strategy worked.

During that period of my life, my world shrank to two places: school and Skateland. That was it. I didn't have friends to play with—not because I didn't want them, but because I didn't have the time or permission. I didn't spend time with extended family. There were no sleepovers, no weekends at grandparents' houses, no breaks from responsibility. My mother, David, and I were all isolated—each of us carrying our own version of the same loneliness.

Looking back, that isolation was as damaging as anything else. It stripped away support systems quietly and efficiently, leaving us dependent on the very environment that was harming us. And when you're a child, you don't have the words to name it—you just feel the absence. The silence. The narrowing of your world.

Those lost Saturday nights weren't just missed church services. They were the loss of connection, protection, and a reminder that love could exist without conditions. And their absence left a void that would echo for years.

That period of my life was immeasurably damaging.

Alongside the isolation, I vividly remember the countless arguments between my mother and father. David and I would run upstairs to our bedrooms, hearts pounding, while downstairs we could hear objects breaking—glass, furniture, pieces of a life shattering one sound at a time. Those noises didn't just echo through the house; they lodged themselves in our nervous systems.

One incident in particular still stands out. My mother threw a candlestick at my father. All these years later, I still possess those candlesticks. And I'll tell you this without exaggeration: if that candlestick had struck my father in the right place, my visits afterward would have been split between a cemetery and a prison. That is how close things came to irreversible tragedy.

For years after that night, there was a dent in the refrigerator where the candlestick finally landed. It remained there like a scar—silent, unmoving, but impossible to ignore. Every time I saw it, it reminded me of just how volatile and dangerous that time had been.

My father would often say, *"What would it have been like if your mother had stayed?"*

I know the answer to that question. If everything else had remained the same, it would not have been good. Not for any of us.

After my brother's book was released, many people approached my mother and asked her, *"Why did you stay?"* People always seem to have solutions in hindsight. They speak as if my mother didn't know what she was doing, as if she hadn't weighed every option, every fear, every possible outcome. It all circles back to what I discussed earlier about preservation.

Good parents try to preserve a family.

That's what my mother was doing. She wasn't naïve. She wasn't weak. She was trying to save what she loved. In retrospect, what existed then barely resembled a family at all. But when you're inside the moment, you don't see it that way. You're not thinking in clean lines or neat conclusions—you're acting on instinct, hope, and fear.

I've watched footage of the Kennedy assassination countless times. One image has always stayed with me: Jacqueline Kennedy climbing onto the back of the car after her husband was shot, reaching out and grabbing fragments of his skull, desperately trying to put them back together. Any rational person knows that couldn't work. But trauma doesn't operate on logic. In the height of shock and devastation, the mind searches frantically for *any* way to fix the unfixable.

Looking back at my family in 1982 and 1983, I see the same thing. That family had already been assassinated. It was gone. But my mother—like Mrs. Kennedy—tried with everything she had to put it back together. Not because it made sense, but because love doesn't surrender easily. And when something you cherish is dying in front of you, rationality often takes a back seat to desperate hope.

That doesn't make her foolish. It makes her human.

People often ask me how I could have gone back to live with my father—and how I could have forgiven Janice. I'll answer those questions in far greater detail in later chapters, but for now, here is the short answer.

As a middle-aged man—one who has been married almost as many times as I've voted for president—I can say this with clarity and experience: Janice was acting on the cues my father gave her. She did not create the chaos; she operated within the permission structure he established. My father could have ended all of this immediately. At any point. But he didn't.

Janice was an opportunist. Plain and simple. She had nothing to lose. Yes, a family was involved. Yes, a home was

108 | P a g e

destroyed. But if the man who was supposed to protect that home didn't give a damn about preserving it, why should she have?

That may sound harsh, but it's honest.

Responsibility begins with the person who holds the power—and in this situation, that was my father. He set the rules. He blurred the lines. He allowed the damage to continue. Janice merely took advantage of what was already broken.

In the past two chapters, I've talked about my mother and how hard she worked to protect David and me from what was really happening behind the scenes of what appeared, on the outside, to be an idyllic family. She shielded us as best she could from the truth, from the betrayals, from the fractures forming beneath the surface. For a time, that protection worked—at least enough to preserve the illusion.

But illusions don't last forever.

Eventually, the curtain gets pulled back. And when it does, the hardest part isn't accepting what others did—it's coming to terms with who had the power to stop it and chose not to

By the time I was twelve years old, I had already developed a deeply cynical view of family. Looking back, it's striking how the early 1980s seemed to produce an entire generation that shared that same skepticism. It wasn't just what was happening inside our homes—it was what we were being fed culturally.

Even popular entertainment reflected it. The number-one television show at the time was Dallas, and the so-called star of the show was J.R. Ewing. J.R. was a man who swindled fellow businessmen, betrayed family members, and carried on affairs while a beautiful wife waited at home. People loved to say he was *"the man you love to hate."*

I'm going to throw the bullshit flag on that.

The truth is, a whole lot of middle-aged men at that time didn't hate J.R. Ewing at all—they admired him. He had money, power, women, and no apparent consequences. He was the embodiment of selfish success, and society rewarded him for it.

I saw how that mindset played out in real life.

When I was about fourteen and living in Brazil, Indiana, we stayed in an apartment complex on Pinckley Street. I remember riding my bike home from my paper route one afternoon and seeing a friend's father kissing one of the tenants. That tenant was not his wife. When he noticed me watching, he didn't panic—he negotiated. He asked me, flat out, *"What's it going to take to keep you quiet?"*

I gave him my price.

He paid it.

About six years later, I ran into that same friend's sister and asked how the family was doing. She told me her mother had left her father for another man. I remember laughing to myself—not because it was funny, but because of the irony. The bill always comes due.

The music of the 1980s wasn't much better. We slow-danced at junior high dances to Careless Whisper by George Michael and WHAM!—a song entirely about infidelity and regret, dressed up as romance. Then there was Part-Time Lover by Stevie Wonder, which practically offered instructions on how to cheat and keep it hidden.

And then came As We Lay by Shirley Murdock. I'll say this: if you actually listen to the lyrics, that song should be titled *As We Gaslight*. She sings about cheating with her best friend's man and then has the audacity to say, *"I would never really want to hurt her/she would never understand."*

Woman—I don't even understand.

The song is framed as if the affair were an accident. Let me be clear: you don't accidentally cheat. Cheating is an intentional act. An accident is leaving your lunchbox on your desk at work and not realizing it until you get home. To test my theory, go home and tell your spouse you *"accidentally"* fell into their best friend's bed. Let me know if they respond with, *"It's okay—accidents happen."*

With all the societal messages of the 1980s—and all the dysfunction happening inside so many homes—it's not surprising that so many people between the ages of forty-five and sixty have been married multiple times. In many ways, it feels like our generation never stood a chance. We were raised in an era that normalized betrayal, romanticized selfishness, and confused desire with entitlement.

By the time we were old enough to question it, the damage had already been modeled for us—on television screens, on dance floors, and, tragically, in our own living rooms.

Another lesson I learned during that time was this: never look back.

My mother and father separated in 1977, and in hindsight, it should have stayed that way. I remember my father telling me that when my mother left in 1977, he told her he was never getting rid of Janice—that he was never going to allow himself to be left alone like that again. What he didn't realize—or perhaps refused to admit—was that in making that decision, he was quietly setting the stage for 1983.

So many of us long for the *"old days."* We romanticize them. We soften the edges of memory and forget the reasons we left in the first place. There's a reason we're warned against that impulse. In the book of Genesis, God warned Lot and his family not to look back as Sodom and Gomorrah were being destroyed. Lot's wife did exactly that—she looked back, longing for what once was—and she was turned into a pillar of salt.

That story isn't about punishment; it's about attachment. Looking back freezes you. It traps you in a moment that no longer exists and keeps you from moving forward.

Going back to a situation—whether personal or professional—is more often than not a mistake. Even listening to my father explain *why* he kept Janice is reason enough to understand that. When you leave something, there is always a reason. Time may dull the pain, but it doesn't erase the truth. And if you do go back, remember this: you have changed, but the situation usually hasn't. Whatever made you leave the first time will resurface, often louder and more destructive than before.

I've been married and divorced multiple times, but one thing I never considered was going back. Not because I couldn't—but because it was never an option in my mind. Forward was the only direction that made sense.

There's a quote attributed to Abraham Lincoln that has always stuck with me: *"I may walk slowly, but I never walk backward."* Of all the wisdom Lincoln shared, that may be one of the most powerful. Progress doesn't require speed—it requires direction.

Too often, when people go back, the second separation is far uglier than the first. More resentment. More damage. More clarity that should have come earlier. Looking back rarely gives you what you're hoping for—it usually just reminds you why you left.

Sometimes the bravest thing you can do isn't reconciliation. It's remembering, learning, and choosing not to repeat what already broke you.

A couple of chapters ago, I told you about us running through the neighborhood of Fox on Farms, trying to leave. I remember that moment vividly—and I remember missing my father deeply, even as everything was unraveling. My father says it was August 10. My mother says it was August 14. Both of them insist it's a day they will never forget—though clearly one of them forgot the exact date.

But the date doesn't matter nearly as much as the *finality* of that moment. What I remember most is the totality of how we left.

There was no slow transition. No long goodbye. My mother told my brother and me to pack whatever we could and put it in the car. At the time, she owned a 1981 Volvo DL.

That car became our lifeboat. Everything we could take—physically and emotionally—had to fit inside it.

I remember my father saying to my mother, *"If you leave, there will be a white Mazda RX-7 in this driveway tonight."* Janice owned that car. The older I get, the more I question why he thought that statement would be an incentive to stay. It wasn't an apology. It wasn't a plea. It was a flex. And it said far more about his priorities than he probably realized.

We packed what we could. We had a bike rack, but it could only hold two bikes—my brother's and mine. My mother had a bike as well, but my father said, *"That bike stays."* And so it did.

About twenty-five years later, my dad told me to take that bike and give it back to my mother. When I finally told her that I still had her bike after all those years, she looked at me and said she didn't want it.

That response stayed with me.

To me, it was clear: my mother didn't look back. Not emotionally. Not symbolically. That bike belonged to a chapter she had already closed. Her refusal wasn't bitterness—it was resolve.

My daughters rode that bike for years, until they each left the house and built lives of their own. Eventually, the bike made its way to a Goodwill in Indianapolis. Somewhere out there, someone is riding it right now—completely unaware of the history it carries.

And I can't help but smile at that.

If they knew the stories behind that bike—the arguments, the ultimatums, the leaving, the not looking back—they would be astonished. To them, it's just a bike. To me, it's a reminder that sometimes the most ordinary objects quietly bear witness to the most extraordinary moments of survival.

Anyway, on that day in August of 1983, once the car was packed as full as it could possibly be, my mother, my brother, and I got in and pulled away. I remember turning around and looking through the rear window and seeing my father following us. He stayed behind us all the way to the Kensington Expressway. Then, at that point, he had to make a choice: does he continue to follow us, or does he turn off and go to Skateland?

He chose Skateland.

Even though I wasn't in Buffalo that night to see it with my own eyes, I'm confident that there was, in fact, a white Mazda RX-7 sitting in the driveway. That detail feels inevitable now—less a question and more a punctuation mark on everything that had already been decided.

On our drive to Indiana, the old, reliable Volvo betrayed us. It blew a head gasket somewhere along the way. I still remember looking back and seeing thick black smoke pouring out of the rear of the car. We ended up stranded and had to sleep in a conference room in Erie, Pennsylvania, waiting for a car dealership to open so the vehicle could be repaired. Even our escape came with obstacles.

Anyone who knows me knows that I love cars. I've owned many over the years, but two brands have always stood out— Volvo and Cadillac. I've come to realize that attachment traces back to this period of my life. I suppose I trust machines more than people. A car can fail you honestly. When it breaks, it tells you. People tend to hurt you quietly, then explain it away later.

You'll see in future chapters that this separation—though absolutely necessary—created an entirely new set of problems and circumstances. Trauma doesn't disappear when you leave a place; it just changes shape. But there's no denying that 1983 made me a different person. The closeness I once had with my father vanished during that time. I was angry with him—deeply angry. And on top of that, I had no idea that an enormous culture shock was waiting for me just around the corner.

Years later, as I watched my father lying in a hospital bed, looking at me and asking that I tell my mother he was sorry, it was the first time I had ever heard him ask for forgiveness. That took courage. Real courage. But what took even more courage was what followed.

My mother forgave him.

That moment remains one of the most powerful things I have ever witnessed her do—and she has done many great things in her life. That act of forgiveness didn't erase the past, but it changed the future. It showed me that forgiveness isn't weakness; it's strength under control. And in many ways, it planted the seed for how I would later choose to forgive others in my own life.

That day in August didn't just mark an ending. It marked the beginning of who I would become—shaped by loss, forged by anger, and forever changed by the road we took away from Buffalo.

What finally stopped my father from talking about my mother that afternoon was the Buffalo Bills game coming on. As we had done every Sunday while my dad was sick, we settled in to watch it together. It was 2013, and the Bills still weren't very good. Some things, apparently, never change.

After the Bills lost—as they often did—I got up and started getting ready to head back to Indiana. Janice was in the hospital room at the time, and she stood up to walk me to the elevator. As I was heading toward the door, my father looked at me and said, *"Are you coming back on Friday?"*

I replied, *"Yes."*

He paused, then said, *"Please do, because if you don't come back, I will cry."*

I looked at him and smiled slightly, almost reflexively, and said, *"Okay,"* assuming he was being a little dramatic. But as I continued walking toward the elevator, he stopped me again and said, more firmly this time, that he was serious. He wasn't joking. He really meant it.

That moment stayed with me as I left the hospital.

As I walked out, I realized something profound: the man I knew in 1983 was already gone. That version of my father—the one defined by control, distance, and chaos—had died long before this hospital room. The man lying in that bed was someone else entirely. He was a man reckoning with his past, someone working—perhaps for the first time—to confront and correct the errors that had made life so difficult for the last thirty years.

There was humility there. Vulnerability. And a quiet urgency to make amends while time still allowed it.

Watching him that day, I understood that people don't always change when it's convenient. Sometimes they change when there is nothing left to hide behind. And sometimes, the bravest thing a man can do is admit—without excuses, without defensiveness—that he got it wrong and wishes he had done better.

That realization didn't erase the past, but it reframed it. And it marked the beginning of a different kind of relationship—one shaped not by who he had been, but by who he was trying, in his final chapters, to become.

Chapter 7

You Do You

During the time my father was sick, life did not pause. I was still working on my dissertation, carrying two very different weights at the same time—one academic, one deeply personal.

While my father slept, I would sit nearby with my laptop open, chipping away at paragraphs, footnotes, and research citations. Sometimes he would sleep for an hour at a time, and during those quiet windows I would squeeze in as much studying as my tired mind would allow. The room would be still, broken only by the hum of the laptop and the rhythm of his breathing.

There was one moment I will never forget. I lifted my head from the screen after typing for a while and noticed my father was awake, watching me. Instinctively, I stopped typing, saved my work, and began to close my laptop. Without saying a word at first, he shook his head gently—no, keep going. Then he spoke, calmly but firmly, and said, *"Just keep doing what you're doing. You still have a life to live."*

I looked at him and smiled, then replied, *"Right now, I'd rather spend time with you. Besides, my eyes are going cross from all this nonprofit research."* He paused for a moment, staring off as if he were somewhere far away, revisiting a version of himself long gone. Then he said quietly, almost to himself, *"I really should've gotten my college degree."*

That statement hit me harder than he probably realized. My father was extremely smart—brilliant, really. He could have been anything he wanted to be if circumstances, choices, and timing had aligned differently. Ironically, he once told me he was voted *"least likely to succeed"* in high school. That label could not have been more wrong. The truth is, he succeeded in ways that couldn't be measured by diplomas or titles. He built businesses, raised children, survived storms, and left an imprint on everyone who truly knew him.

And here's the funny thing about the Goggins family: if you really want to guarantee our success, just tell us we're going to fail. That challenge lights a fire every single time. It always has.

My father was a very successful businessman, but success did not shield him from complicated relationships. He often shared stories about his so-called friends in East Amherst— men who were present in his life, sometimes even helpful, yet rarely fair to him. On the surface, they appeared loyal. They showed up when he needed a hand or a conversation. But beneath that surface, the relationship was transactional and uneven.

He told me how these men would regularly come to him with investment ideas, always dressed up as *"can't-miss opportunities."* What he noticed over time, though, was a troubling pattern. The truly safe, sure-thing investments were quietly kept out of his reach. Those were reserved for others. But when it came to high-risk ventures—the kind that required capital and optimism—they were more than happy to include him and, more importantly, his money.

I remember him talking about investing in oil wells in Michigan, fish farms, and a handful of other ventures that sounded promising at the time but never quite delivered. He didn't lose everything, but he also didn't gain much of anything. What he really lost was time—years spent trusting people who saw him less as a friend and more as a financial resource.

They did my father wrong. There's no softer way to say it. And yet, in true Goggins fashion, he found ways to get them back—not through confrontation or revenge, but by outlasting them, by succeeding in other arenas, and by refusing to let their behavior define his worth. The whole thing was the strangest *"friendship"* you could imagine.

Looking back, I don't believe it was rooted in camaraderie at all. It was a relationship born out of necessity—for them, for access; for him, for connection. It functioned, but it was hollow. There was proximity, but no brotherhood. Presence, but no loyalty. And that distinction mattered more than any failed investment ever could.

As I watched my father, a realization settled in that I couldn't shake. In Buffalo, he was the king of the street—respected, known, and grounded in a world that understood him. Yet at the same time, he fought diligently to maintain what felt like a fragile citizenship in the suburbs of Western New York. It was as if he lived in two worlds at once, never fully belonging to either, constantly adjusting his posture just to remain accepted.

My father was not alone in this struggle. What he lived through is part of a much larger crisis—one that affects far more people than we are willing to admit. It isn't necessarily a crisis of color; it's a crisis of class. People who are moving up the ladder quickly learn that progress comes with invisible rules. You have to be careful—careful at work, careful in your neighborhoods, careful about the words you use at home and the ones you don't say at all. Every environment requires a different version of you, and the cost of getting it wrong can be high.

It's a delicate balance to maintain. And the irony is cruel. When you start to climb, the people you're moving away from often think you believe you're too good for them now. Meanwhile, the people you think you're moving closer to quietly—or sometimes openly—decide you're still not good enough. You exist in the space between judgment and expectation, belonging nowhere completely.

For us, that balance played out every single weekend—one foot in the street, one foot in the suburbs. Even for my sisters and me, it was a constant negotiation of identity. We learned early how to code-switch without realizing that's what we were doing. How to be tough but polite, confident but not threatening, ambitious but not arrogant.

At its core, this struggle to fit in goes beyond race. It cuts across class, opportunity, and access. It's the quiet burden carried by those who are trying to build a better life while still honoring where they came from. And watching my father navigate that tightrope taught me just how exhausting—and how courageous—that balancing act really is.

In my brother's book *Can Hurt Me*, he wrote openly about his struggles with racism in Brazil, Indiana. What followed was almost predictable. He caught a lot of flak from local residents who were quick to insist that racism didn't exist there at all. That denial, in itself, was telling. The truth is, racism did exist—but for the people who already fit in, who were never questioned or challenged by the system, it was easy to claim it wasn't real. You don't feel a problem when you're never the one carrying it.

I remember my own time living in Indiana, when I was still new to the city and learning the unspoken rules. One day, I said something in front of a group that included some Black kids and one White kid. The white kid got visibly upset. I noticed—but I didn't care. After he walked away, one of the Black kids pulled me aside and said quietly, *"We don't say that here."* He went on to explain that saying things like that would make people angry, and that anger could turn into something worse for me.

I understood what he was really saying. He wasn't correcting my words—he was trying to protect me. He was explaining survival. But the truth was, I didn't care. I was going to say what I wanted to say. I wasn't going to shrink myself, soften my voice, or become submissive just to make other people comfortable over something that made no sense to me.

Those kids—the Black kids especially—were struggling to fit in. I could see it clearly. And in my own way, I wanted to fit in too. But I was from a different place, shaped by a different environment, and I already knew something important: fitting in at the cost of your dignity isn't fitting in at all. It's surrender.

I wasn't reckless, but I also wasn't willing to live by rules rooted in fear or enforced by unspoken threats. I refused to back down for the sake of a false peace or a stupid purpose. That moment stayed with me—not because of what I said, but because it revealed how early we learn the difference between belonging and survival, and how often people are forced to choose between the two.

I remember that even in the schools in Brazil, Indiana, there were moments that made it painfully clear I was different—and not in a way that felt celebrated or safe. One teacher in particular made comments that left me deeply uncomfortable, though at the time I didn't yet have the language to fully name why.

One weekend, my father came down to visit me. He arrived in his 1962 Rolls-Royce Silver Cloud—a car that turned heads wherever it went. In a small town like Brazil, people noticed. The following week in class, that same teacher looked at me and said, in front of everyone, *"Is that your dad's Rolls-Royce? What is he, a pimp?"*

The room erupted in laughter. I didn't.

I felt a heat rise in my chest—anger, embarrassment, disbelief—all at once. I told him plainly that my father was a businessman in Buffalo, New York, and that he made a lot of money. But the damage had already been done. The fact that his mind went immediately to *"pimp"* said far more about him than it ever could about my father. Still, I was the one left sitting there, exposed, singled out, and humiliated.

This was the same teacher who used to call me *"Chocolate Thunder."* At the time, he brushed it off as harmless—a nickname borrowed from a basketball player whose name I can't even remember now. The irony was thick. I didn't like basketball, I wasn't even that dark-skinned, and yet he felt perfectly comfortable labeling his only Black student with a racially loaded nickname and calling it good taste.

What made it worse was that the subject he taught genuinely interested me. I cared about it. I was engaged. But because of him—because of his ignorance, his careless words, his willingness to turn me into a punchline—I completely lost interest. The following year, I didn't take the course at all. Even now, I'm angry about that. Angry that I allowed someone else's ignorance to steal something I truly enjoyed.

To defend myself—or at least what I thought was defending myself—I turned to self-deprecating humor. Around that time, Eddie Murphy had done a Buckwheat skit on *Saturday Night Live*, and I remember walking around mimicking it. People laughed. That laughter felt like armor. Even my grandmother—my mother's mother—told me to stop doing it. I didn't understand why back then. I thought it was funny. I thought I was in control.

Now I see it clearly.

What I was really doing was belittling myself before anyone else could. I was shrinking myself, turning myself into a caricature, hoping humor would dull the sting of prejudice. It didn't. It only reinforced it. I wasn't protecting myself—I was slowly eroding my own dignity, one laugh at a time.

That realization didn't come until much later. But it remains one of the hardest lessons I had to learn: sometimes the most damaging harm isn't just what others say to you— it's what you learn to say about yourself just to survive.

Even with all of that being said, I don't want to give the impression that Brazil, Indiana, was nothing more than a racist town. That wouldn't be fair, and it wouldn't be true. There were—and still are—some genuinely good people there. People who welcomed me, stood by me, and became deep, lifelong friends. Many of them remain dear to me to this day, and their stories deserve to be told as well. This book will include those moments, too, because the truth is always more complicated than a single narrative.

As I grew older, I came to understand something important: racism comes in at least two distinct forms. There is what I call *red-state racism* and *blue-state racism*. The racism I experienced in Brazil, Indiana, was unmistakably red-state racism—it was loud, direct, and in your face. You didn't have to guess where you stood. The lines were clear, even when they were ugly.

But in the clean, manicured suburbs of East Amherst, New York, I encountered a different kind altogether—blue-state racism. This version was quieter, polished, and wrapped in plausible deniability. It lived in whispers, assumptions, and casual remarks spoken without fear because the speaker believed they were among *"their own."*

I remember one moment vividly while sitting in class at Williamsville East High School. Two girls were talking in front of me about a party that had happened over the weekend—one I hadn't attended. One girl leaned toward the other and said, *"Do you realize so-and-so fucked a Black guy?"*

The words hit me like a slap.

In that instant, I understood exactly what she meant. To her, sleeping with a Black man wasn't just notable—it was degrading. It carried the same tone one might use to describe sleeping with someone diseased or untouchable. In her mind, Black people weren't equals; we were something to be avoided, something lesser, something *other*.

Right after she said it, her friend gasped and whispered, *"Oh my gosh—Trunnis is right behind you."*

The girl turned around, visibly embarrassed, scrambling to explain herself. *"Oh, you know what I mean,"* she said nervously. *"I mean, I would never fuck a Black guy... I mean, you know."*

And I did know.

I looked at her and replied calmly, *"Oh, I totally understand—because most of the Black guys I know would never fuck you."*

The entire class erupted in laughter.

Both of us were sent to the principal's office. The vice principal did nothing—no lecture, no accountability, no acknowledgment of what had actually happened. We were simply told to *"watch our language,"* as if the issue were profanity and not prejudice.

But in that moment, something shifted inside me. I knew, right then and there, that self-deprecating humor was no longer going to be my shield. I was done shrinking myself to make other people comfortable. If I didn't fit in, then I didn't fit in. That was fine.

What was no longer acceptable was sacrificing my self-respect just to belong.

That day marked the end of one survival strategy and the beginning of another. I wasn't going to laugh at myself anymore so others wouldn't have to confront their ignorance. From that point forward, I chose dignity over acceptance— and I've never regretted that decision.

For those of you wondering what I mean when I talk about *red-state racism* and *blue-state racism*, let me be clear.

Red-state racism is rooted in fear—fear that the opposing race is a threat. And oddly enough, embedded in that fear is a kind of twisted respect. You don't see someone as a threat unless you believe they are your equal or, in some cases, even stronger than you. To acknowledge a threat is to acknowledge power. It's ugly, it's wrong, but it is direct. You know where you stand.

Blue-state racism operates very differently. It isn't loud or confrontational. It's quiet, polished, and often cloaked in self-righteousness. In this version, you're not seen as a threat— you're seen as a burden. You are viewed as someone beneath them, someone whose survival depends on their generosity, patience, or *"enlightenment."* They speak *about* you as if you're not even in the room, and they speak *to* you as if you couldn't possibly know what's best for yourself.

That kind of racism is harder to confront because it disguises itself as concern.

I'll never forget a conversation I had in my 50s with a white man in his 30s. We were talking about race, and at some point, he said, *"Based on a book I read, this is what you're encountering, and as a result, you need to be mindful of what's happening to you."*

I remember staring at him for a moment before responding. Then I said, *"Buddy, I've been Black since before you were born. And now, because you've read one book, you suddenly know exactly what I need to do to survive this life?"*

I paused and added, *"That is probably one of the most racist things I've ever heard."*

He looked stunned.

"It's racist," I continued, *"because you think you know what's best for me—and you have absolutely no clue."*

That moment crystallized something for me. Blue-state racism doesn't shout slurs or issue threats. It assumes authority. It places itself above you morally and intellectually, then hands down guidance you never asked for. It robs you of agency while congratulating itself for being progressive.

I'm certain what my father endured decades earlier was far worse than anything I've described here. The margins were tighter, the consequences harsher, and the room for error much smaller. Still, the balancing act remains. Many minorities living in suburban spaces—then and now—are forced to navigate this same tension.

Whether intentional or unintentional, this dynamic makes you feel out of place. And it's not just about race. It's also about class. About access. About proximity to power. People climbing ladders—socially, economically, professionally—are constantly adjusting themselves, trying to exist without offending, threatening, or disappointing anyone.

That balance is exhausting. And once you see it clearly, you realize it's not something you imagined—it's something you've been carrying all along.

I see that struggle far too often.

Working in the community college system, I encounter many first-generation college students—young men and women taking courageous steps to move beyond the circumstances they were born into. They are pushing against gravity, against expectations, and against unspoken rules that tell them who they are supposed to remain. Once again, that familiar tension appears: being perceived as *too good* for some, while still being seen as *not good enough* for others. It's a daily fight many of them carry quietly.

I once had a student who lived in a trailer park in southern Indiana. Her father had passed away, and despite the weight of that loss, she was determined to break into the banking industry. She was a phenomenal student—disciplined, focused, and relentless in her work ethic. Her drive didn't just transform her own life; it inspired her younger sister to raise her grades and dream bigger as well.

Any time there was an opportunity to place her in a leadership role—whether in the classroom, a business club, or a professional development setting—I made sure she was considered. Not as a favor, but because she earned it. I nominated her for Business Student of the Year, and she won. I still remember standing at the awards ceremony when she proudly introduced me to her family—her mother, her uncle, and her sister.

When I extended my hand to shake her uncle's, he looked at me and said, *"So you're the one who took our girl away."*

I was stunned.

This young woman wasn't being taken away—she was blazing a path. She was becoming proof that it could be done. What he saw as loss, I saw as legacy. Still, I understood the fear beneath his words. Success can feel like abandonment to those who've never been invited to imagine it.

I'm certain that to this day, she still struggles to balance her life in banking with her ties to home. Progress often comes with guilt, and ambition can be misread as betrayal. On a brighter note, her sister went on to graduate from college as well and is now a nurse. I am immensely proud of both of those young women. I'm also painfully aware of the quiet battles they continue to fight.

On the flip side, I remember sitting in a leadership meeting at that same college—a discussion focused on campus security and whether anything needed to be improved. When one of the senior leaders was asked if there were any concerns, she responded dismissively, saying, "I can't think of anything. Nothing bad has ever happened to me, so in my opinion, we're fine."

As she said it, she looked directly at me—the only Black person in the room, and the only one who had a daughter who was murdered.

Her expression was smug.

For a brief moment, anger surged through me. Then I paused and considered the source. When it was my turn to speak, my response was raw and unapologetic. I said, *"Just because it hasn't happened to you doesn't mean it won't. And if you're not prepared for it when it does happen, it will happen far worse."*

That moment permanently strained our professional relationship. But I don't regret what I said. What troubled me most wasn't the tension—it was the realization that if someone like her spoke that way to a student like the young woman I described earlier, that student might shrink. She might second-guess herself. She might decide not to move forward because she wasn't insulated by the privilege others take for granted.

That sense of not belonging can quietly convince people to stay exactly where they are.

This is why I believe people in leadership—especially in educational institutions—must be mindful of their words. I won't use the phrase *"check your privilege."* It's overused and often weaponized. But I will say this: do everything in your power to build people up. Be intentional about creating spaces where hard-working individuals feel welcomed, seen, and supported.

And for those of us who are trying to fit in, remember this truth: there are people who offer advice and make suggestions not for *your* benefit, but for *their* comfort. Learn to recognize the difference. Your growth may unsettle others—but that does not mean you are wrong for growing.

Your advancement—your hard work, your growth, and your success—can make other people deeply uncomfortable.

And when that happens, they may try to discourage you from moving forward, not because your path is wrong, but because it disrupts their sense of comfort.

I'll never forget when I first released *The 4Ps of You*. A colleague offered his congratulations, then immediately followed it with, *"Don't you have to go on a book tour? Man, I would hate to go from hotel to hotel to hotel."* I remember looking at him and replying, *"Well, I'm glad* you *don't have to go from hotel to hotel to hotel."*

Then he added, *"Well, you won't be able to play hockey anymore."*

And he was right.

I don't play hockey nearly as much as I used to. It's a sport I love. But the truth is, my passion for writing books—and the impact those books can have—far outweighs playing beer-league hockey on Thursday nights. That wasn't really the point, though. Those weren't genuine concerns for *me*. They were subtle signals meant to say, *Weren't you comfortable where you were? You had a good thing. Now you're changing your position and your status—and while it may benefit you, it makes me uncomfortable.*

That realization hit home.

My father lived life his own way, yet it still surprises me how much he cared about what other people thought of him. The Rolls-Royce, the big houses, the lavish dinners—it's taken me years to understand that much of that wasn't really for him. It was for the people around him. It was proof. It was presentation. It was armor.

My father was deeply concerned with how he was perceived.

One of the most important lessons I learned from watching his extravagance was this: as long as *I* like me, I'm okay. In fact, the more I genuinely like and respect myself, the more the right people around me will do the same.

And make no mistake—there are people around you right now who do not like you. There always will be. If you walked on water tomorrow, they'd tell everyone you don't know how to swim. Those people are never going to like you. Don't waste your time trying to impress them.

Work hard on building what *you* want to build. Be the person *you* want to be. Live in a way that aligns with your values, not someone else's comfort.

I often wonder how different my father's life might have been if he had truly focused on what *he* thought about himself, rather than what he wanted others to think about him. I can say this with certainty: he would have been a much happier man.

That lesson didn't come cheaply—but it was worth learning.

Chapter 8

Culture Shock

It was another late Sunday afternoon, and I was on my way home to Indianapolis. What was so ironic was I was on that very interstate in which Volvo blew a head gasket. This time 30 years later, I was in a reliable 2012 Ford Escape. For the first time in 30 years, I received a sense of closure regarding the events of 1983. I guess dad finally admitting that the situation could've been handled differently was something I really needed to stop thinking about the heart ache and pain associated with those events. The other thing that I found so ironic about driving on this highway was that out of all of the things that happen over the past 30 years, it was me and my immediate family and me being the only ones still living in Indiana.

Even more ironic, other than my father, I adamantly did not want to live in Indiana. Nothing against the state of Indiana, but I'm a Buffaloian through and through. I really am a Buffalo snob when it comes to pizza. I'm probably going to offend a lot of my readers when I say this, but Buffalo New York has by far the best pizza on the planet. I can name many pizzerias in that area that are great, but quite frankly, I do not have enough pages for this book to describe all of the greatness of Buffalo pizza. In addition to the pizza, hockey is very popular in Buffalo.

Though I did play hockey in Indianapolis as an adult, I remember long ago when I lived in Brazil, Indiana, I stopped playing hockey because there was no ice rink anywhere to be found. As a matter of fact, when I moved with my mother to Brazil, Indiana, in 1983, I suffered quite the culture shock. We moved in August, so school was about ready to start soon after we arrived. My seventh-grade year was at Brazil Junior High School. The junior high and high school were actually one in the same. The buildings were very old at the time (they have now opened newer buildings and changed the name of the school). In addition, the school was an open campus, and I remember for lunch walking into *"town"* with my friend Chad Herron.

Chad was the first person I met when I came to Brazil, Indiana. He and his family went to church at Annunciation Catholic. My grandmother was a devout Catholic, and by default, as long as I lived around my grandmother, so was I.

We lived with my grandmother for a very short time, moving to Brazil. My grandmother and grandfather played a key role in the stabilization of our family after my mother moved to Indiana. Their example that they presented to me in 1983 now serves as the foundation of how I approach my grandchildren today.

Though my grandchildren never met my grandparents, they do have a lot to thank my grandparents for. Anyway, Brazil Junior High School was different, to say the least. When I was living in Buffalo and going to Mill Middle School, most of those kids I knew grew up with me. I was never any different than they were. However, when I went to Brazil Junior High School, I was quickly reminded that I was different. I had many differences to my new schoolmates.

First, my favorite sport was hockey, and for most of the kids I went to school in Brazil, their favorite sport was basketball. People in Indiana are obsessed with that sport. I never liked it. I think one of the reasons why I don't like it is because you cannot check someone into the boards and basketball. As a matter fact, it seems like just the mere touch of your opponent in basketball leads to a foul. I truly think the beautiful violence of hockey is what's missing in the sport of basketball.

Second difference I had was the fact that I had a Buffalo, New York, accent. I was far and away not a Hoosier. Third was the music that I listened to. I grew up in Skateland around funk music, and rap music was growing. Groups like Run DMC, the Sugar Hill Gang, and Grandmaster Flash were my favorite groups at the time. The people in Brazil, Indiana, at that time never heard of them. You've got to remember this is long before YouTube and the Internet; music was very regional at the time. Also, during this time, Def Leppard was the group that everybody in Brazil seemed to like. Every time I hear the song by Def Leppard *"Rock of Ages,"* I can't help but think about my first couple of months in Brazil, Indiana.

Finally, the primary difference that I had with my schoolmates in Brazil, Indiana, was the color of my skin. For the first time in my entire life, the color of my skin was a point of conversation. It did lead to some very uncomfortable moments. Those uncomfortable moments were not only with students but with teachers as well. I remember the first time in which a girl told me that she liked me, but she couldn't hang out with me because I was black and her father would get very upset if he knew we were talking.

Yes, it was a different time then, but even to this day, I remember the effects of the subtle racism that I experienced at a young age. Also, when it came to race, the other black kids (and there weren't many) would tell me how to *"behave"* around the other white people in Brazil. I'll still never forget I said something to a white kid at the public park in Brazil, and after the exchange, one of the black kids came to me and said, *We don't say that here. You can get in trouble.* I looked at him and said *I'm gonna say whatever I want to say.*

One thing about racism is it will always exist, but if confronted properly, will always take a backseat to respect and integrity. All races have racial bias.

Whenever you are faced with that racism, always remember that you are human first and you demand respect. I have never considered myself a victim of racism. I've always considered myself a warrior against racism. The best way to end racism is to never be a victim of racism, always be a combatant. Though there was a culture shock, there were things that happened in Brazil, Indiana, that affect my life today in a positive way. One of which is the McAfoos family. I met the son, TJ, at the park pool shortly after I moved to Brazil, Indiana.

Remember all the things that I went through in 1983 kinda made me a loner. I didn't have any friends to speak of my first moved to Brazil. To be honest with you, I really don't think I was looking for friends. TJ swam up to me and just started talking. Quite frankly, at the time, he was extremely annoying. I truly wanted to be left alone.

However, thankfully, TJ was insistent to get to know me. He talked and talked and talked, and finally I started to warm up to him. Not too long after, I went over his house to hang out and I met his family. His mother, Linda, and his dad, Rod, are still two of the kindest people I'll ever meet. Just recently, TJ got remarried, and I was blessed to stand in his wedding. One thing that pleasantly struck me during this wedding ceremony is that Linda and Rod addressed to me as their "*son*".

Frankly, they are part of my family. I always tell everybody that I was Linda and Rod's *"favorite son"*. I have talked about this and other books before, but I will talk about it again. After all that I went through in 1983, my idea of family was literally destroyed, but the McAfoos family restored my faith in the idea of family. You could tell that the three of them loved each other dearly, and that love extended way past the walls and yard of their home. Recently, when I was at TJ's wedding, I saw just how far that love extended.

The McAfoos family basically had me over every single weekend we went on so many adventures together. Those adventures eventually turned into traditions to the family that I eventually had as an adult. You will see in the next chapter how this family actually provided a sense of shelter for me.

There is no amount of gratitude that I can express so that Rod, Linda, and TJ can truly know how much they mean to me. I often think about my state of being after the happenings of 1983. I often think where I could be mentally, or if I would even be at all if that annoying kid TJ did not swim up to me at the park pool. There are times when God sends an angel to save His people. In my case, God sent three angels to the Forest Park swimming pool. I love them all dearly.

Another person I happened to meet in Brazil, Indiana, who changed my life and continues to enrich my life is Dana

Garrett. I met her at the Cooper Theater. Brazil, Indiana, only had one theater that played one movie for one entire week. One Saturday night, I went to the Cooper Theater with my brother and met Dana Garrett and her sister Deanna. We formed an instant friendship. As a matter fact, I remember the four of us talking during the whole movie. We had a blast.

Dana and I often try to remember the movie in which we met each other. Neither one of us know. I'm going to say it's probably because we were talking during the whole movie. Anyway, what made it so unique about the fun time we had was that both of us were in Brazil, Indiana, due to our families breaking up. Though we smiled at each other at the movie theater, both of us went home to fragmented families. The wonderful thing about that is it was not the fragmented families that bonded us; it was just an instant connection.

Now, all these years later, after several pit stops along the way, we are happily married and living in Asheville, North Carolina. As old as we are, it is probably safe to say that we will spend the rest of our lives together. Though the wait was very long and the path was quite treacherous, it is fantastic that I have the opportunity to say that.

Again, I cannot stress enough how instrumental my mother's parents were in helping my mother, my brother, and me begin life anew in Indiana. My mother went back to college in Brazil in her 30s. I remember watching her sit at the kitchen table doing her homework while I sat at the opposite end doing mine.

That scene played a pivotal role in my going on, not only getting my bachelor's degree in my 30s, but getting my PhD in my 40s. As a non-traditional student myself who teaches non-traditional students, I often tell the story of my mother as a single mother raising two boys, going to college full-time. I share this story primarily with women to inspire them to move on during difficult periods in a semester. I know for a fact that that story works.

My brother fell in love with basketball during this time and instantly started playing. I, being *"a hockey player"*, did not play any high school junior high sports. Boy, did I miss hockey. I do remember when my grandmother got cable, and ESPN was a part of the cable package, and I got to watch hockey games once more. However, ice skates and hockey sticks are not a thing in Brazil, Indiana.

Once we got settled in Brazil, I remember thinking of my father and wanting to reach out to him. We went months without speaking to him. He didn't call, but I did miss him. Though I was still angry at him due to the situation, I still wanted to hear his voice. I remember calling him, and we agreed that we would talk to each other every Sunday after Skateland closed. I truly looked forward to that time. Not only did I talk to him, but even David talk to him briefly those Sundays.

The summer after my seventh-grade year, my father and Janice came to pick us up for couple weeks in the summer. It was the first time I had seen my father since August 1983. My father came to Brazil driving the Mercedes 450 SLC. Yes, that was the same Mercedes that he had *"purchased"* for my mother. That car now served a different purpose. I would admit that the parental exchange was more than an awkward moment. As a parent who has had to go through many of those exchanges, I kinda have an understanding of what my mother was feeling during that exchange.

There she is, having to trust the very woman who deceived her so recently to provide some level of maternal care for her children in her absence. Surely that must've been awkward. My father had planned that we were going to meet my sister Teresa at Great Escape Fun Park in Lake George, New York. At one point, my dad got tired of driving and then yielded the steering wheel to Janice. While Janice was driving, we got caught up in traffic on the interstate. We were complaining about the backup, and out of nowhere, David reminded Janice and Dad that the Mercedes 450 SLC used to be his mother's car.

As a 13-year-old who knew the wrath of dad, I believe I was more uncomfortable than David at that moment. I really don't think David realized what may happen to him after his unsolicited statement. What I expected my dad to do at that point, thankfully, he didn't do, but he did emphatically state that language like that will not be tolerated. He also went on to decree the true ownership of that vehicle in its current state. The car was quiet for a little while. It wasn't until the beauty of Lake George could be seen from our car windows that conversation once again started to flow in that car. We went on to have a very exciting summer with Dad that year.

We went up to Canada to visit Janice's family. It's in a town right off Georgian Bay called Owen Sound. I must admit that it is probably one of the prettiest towns in North America. I haven't been up there in quite some time, but every year I long to go back.

It was during that trip we saw the dad that we knew of old. This time instead of lashing out at our mother, David and I saw him lashing out on Janice. During this trip to Owen Sound, my nephew Darnell, who was the same age as David, was with us. Anyway, dad got mad at Janice and left and went back to Buffalo. However, he forgot three things, that was, David, Darnell and me. We spent an entire day after Dad left in Owen Sound, hung out with Janice's family at the park, and finished our vacation. After the day was over, Janice took the three of us back to the United States. I remember Teresa never allowed dad to take Darnell on a trip alone again. The older I get, I am amazed that my dad was bold enough to leave three US citizens in a foreign country virtually on their own with no true parental unit to be there for us if anything were to happen.

We finished that vacation on a high note. During that summer, Michael Jackson was at the height of his success. The Jackson's Victory tour was going through Buffalo. My dad got a chartered bus and invited people from both Skateland and the Vermillion Room to go to the concert. Lisa McNeil even came to this concert. It was so nice seeing her again. I have to say I've been to many concerts after that concert, but there will never be a concert that even comes close to the experience I had at Rich Stadium in 1994 watching the Jacksons perform.

The day after the concert, it was time to go back to Brazil, Indiana. School was getting ready to start again. When we got back to Brazil, my father surprised David and me with a stop at a place called Hughes Honda. Hughes Honda was the place that sold motorcycles, and my father bought us a Honda XL 100 motorcycle.

It was absolutely awesome. I seriously think he bought that not only to win David and I's affection but also to annoy the shit out of my mother. If annoying my mother was part of the plan, it worked. Also, I remember trying to teach my brother how to ride that motorcycle, and to this day, I still have scars on the side of my body due to the fact that he really sucked at riding that thing. Worst thing about it, is that motorcycle almost proved the death of me as well when I had an accident. I still have the fragment of a pebble in my hand because of that motorcycle. I'm not talking ill towards the motorcycle. Quite frankly, I wouldn't mind writing it one more time if I knew where it was.

Anyway, post-1983 life seemed to have become more established. And I was getting used to Brazil Indiana. Seemingly my mother and my father both were getting acclimated to the new lives they had. Finally a sense of normalcy reigned.

Chapter 9

Am I Not "We"

Before getting into this chapter, I must address a question I have been asked many times by Before getting into this chapter, there is something I need to address.

I have been asked—more times than I can count—by people who have read my brother's book, *Why did you turn your back on your mother and your brother?* The short answer is simple and absolute: I didn't. And I never would. Not then. Not now. Not ever.

I've never directly answered that question before. Not publicly, and not in full. But this chapter will provide the clarity that some people have been searching for—especially those who are genuinely trying to understand rather than assign blame.

It was during this period of my life that I truly learned how to be a father. More importantly, I learned hard, uncomfortable lessons about how to navigate broken families and blended families—situations where love, loyalty, resentment, and survival are constantly colliding. What I'm about to share is not a story with heroes and villains neatly defined. It is the story of two entirely selfish men and the consequences of their choices—consequences that did not stop with them, but rippled outward and downward, affecting others across multiple generations.

As I mentioned at the end of the last chapter, there had been a brief sense of normalcy. A fragile equilibrium. Things appeared to be settling, at least on the surface. But then another element entered the equation.

And that's the thing about systems—families included. It only takes one element to change everything.

In chemistry, one part carbon combined with one part oxygen creates carbon monoxide—a silent, deadly gas. But take that same carbon and add *two* parts oxygen, and you get carbon dioxide—something essential for life on Earth. The elements themselves aren't *"bad."* The difference lies in the combination, the balance, and the reaction they create together.

Families work the same way.

It's not always that one person is entirely wrong. Sometimes, it's that the structure itself becomes unstable once a new element is introduced. The composition changes. The reactions change. And what once sustained life can suddenly become toxic.

That is the lens through which this chapter must be read. Not as abandonment. Not as betrayal. But as an honest examination of cause, effect, and the unintended damage that follows when selfishness is allowed to override responsibility.

This is where the story truly begins.

We see this principle play out all the time in sports. I'm a huge Buffalo Sabres fan, and over the past several years I've watched talented players leave the organization—only to go on and win the Stanley Cup with another team. That part, while painful, I can accept.

What really gets to me is this: many of those players were *on the Sabres* during the very years when the team was struggling. The talent was there. The work ethic was there. But something in the environment—the chemistry, the leadership, the structure—was off. It wasn't that the players themselves were the wrong elements. It was the way the elements interacted. The reactions didn't work. And because of that, the whole system failed.

That same principle applied to my life during this period.

A few years back, I did an interview with Eric Carroll for the show Dad Talk. During the conversation, he asked me—point blank—about my relationship with Wilmoth Ervin. Normally, I pride myself on being diplomatic when answering difficult questions. I know how to choose my words carefully. I know how to soften edges.

That day, I didn't.

When I later watched the interview, even I was surprised by how blunt my answer was. I said, without hesitation, *"I didn't like him—and I gave him no reason to want to like me."*

There was no malice in that statement. No theatrics. Just honesty.

Looking back, that response fits perfectly with everything I've learned about systems, families, and relationships. Sometimes things don't work—not because one person is entirely wrong, but because the interaction itself is toxic. The chemistry is off. The environment doesn't allow anyone involved to be their best.

Just like in sports, you can have all the right pieces on the roster—but if the structure is broken, the results will be too.

Our relationship started off on the wrong foot from the very beginning.

I remember the first time he met my brother and me. He asked the usual surface-level questions—what kind of music we liked, what sports we followed, what we watched on television. When it was my turn, I told him plainly that my favorite sport was hockey.

He immediately responded, *"Why don't you like basketball?"*

That question bothered me—not just because of the assumption behind it, but because it wasn't true. I had *never* liked basketball. It wasn't my sport. It never had been. I didn't grow up around it, and I didn't connect with it. I grew up around kids who loved hockey. Hockey was the sport that made sense to me. It was the one I followed, the one I played, the one I cared about.

He then shifted the conversation to the lack of diversity in hockey. To be fair, that observation was true then, and it's still largely true today. But the way he framed it made it feel like my interest in hockey needed justification—as if my identity should dictate my preferences.

At the time, my favorite player was Grant Fuhr, the legendary goaltender for the Edmonton Oilers. Fuhr was my hero. He was the first Black player to win the Stanley Cup, and he had won it the very same year I met Wilmoth. When I pulled his rookie card from a pack of hockey cards, I immediately put it in a protective case. That card still sits in my office to this day.

After being lectured about diversity in hockey, I felt the need—as a kid often does—to *prove* my point. I wanted him to understand that my love for hockey wasn't accidental or ignorant. It was intentional. It was admiration. It was representation. I went to get that hockey card to show him that my favorite player was Black—and not just Black, but great.

When I showed it to him, he dismissed it—or at least, that's how it felt to me. Whether that was his intention or not, the moment landed poorly. What could have been a point of connection instead reinforced the sense that we were never going to see things the same way.

From that very first interaction, it was clear we weren't aligned. The assumptions were wrong. The tone was off. And once that foundation was set, it became difficult—if not impossible—to build anything solid on top of it.

Sometimes relationships don't fall apart dramatically.

Sometimes they simply never get a fair start.

David, on the other hand, got along quite well with Wilmoth. I remember that not long after that initial conversation, I quietly got up and went to my room. I didn't feel comfortable being part of it, and I trusted that instinct. From that point forward, it felt like every interaction I had with him turned into me trying to prove something—about who I was, what I liked, or why I belonged. That's not a foundation for a healthy relationship, and ours never became one.

The introduction of this new element into our family didn't just affect individual relationships—it changed how we all interacted with one another. It shifted the balance in ways that would take years to fully understand.

As Christmas approached, my father wanted David and me to come to Buffalo for the holidays. I was excited to go. David was not. He didn't want to make the trip. My father took that personally. Hurt by David's decision, he bought a plane ticket for me alone and sent me to Buffalo by myself.

What he did next still troubles me.

That year, my father returned all of David's Christmas gifts. With the money, he bought me more expensive ones.

One of those gifts was the Omnibot—a wildly popular and very expensive programmable robot at the time. It cost around five hundred dollars and could do simple things like play music, retrieve drinks, and respond to basic commands. I had wanted one badly, and my father bought it for me. I spent nearly the entire Christmas Day programming that robot, watching it roll across the floor, following my instructions exactly as I had written them.

That was also the Christmas I mentioned earlier—the one where it was just my father and me spending the day together. For reasons I didn't fully understand at the time, he had gotten angry with Janice at Skateland and left her there. So it was just us.

As a child, I remember that day vividly because it felt special. As an adult, I understand that it marked the beginning of something far more troubling.

That Christmas started a pattern—a deeply destructive one.

When David stopped wanting to go to Buffalo, my father responded by doing things *only* for me. When David stopped talking to him during the Sunday evening phone calls, my father slowly stopped trying. Eventually, he didn't even ask how David was doing.

What began as hurt quietly turned into division. And that division was reinforced not by distance alone, but by choices—choices that rewarded one child while emotionally abandoning the other. At the time, I didn't have the maturity to understand the weight of what was happening. I just knew something felt wrong.

Looking back now, I see it clearly: that Christmas wasn't just about gifts or time together. It was the moment favoritism replaced parenting, and silence replaced responsibility. And once that pattern was set, it would echo through our family for years to come.

Wilmoth's reaction to all of this was to swing the pendulum hard in the opposite direction. He began intentionally doing things for David while seemingly—and deliberately—leaving me out. It wasn't subtle. It was pointed.

For example, David played Little League basketball, and one day Wilmoth rented a limousine to take David to a game. A limousine. The message was loud and clear. A few days later, I broke a string on my guitar and needed $1.60 to buy a replacement. I asked to borrow the money because I hadn't collected from my paper route yet. Wilmoth looked at me and said he wasn't going to *"waste his money."*

I still don't fully understand the philosophy behind that kind of behavior. I don't know if it was punishment, leverage, or some warped sense of balance. What I do know is this: I did not deserve that treatment.

Instead of asking *why* this was happening or trying to reason with it, I reacted the only way a kid with no real power knows how—I became rebellious. Quietly at first. Then more openly.

Around that time, there was a band called Duran Duran, and they had a song out called The Reflex. Up until then, I wasn't really a fan. But that guitar riff was catchy, and the song stuck with me. I remember listening to it one day and hearing Wilmoth dismiss it as *"garbage."*

That was all it took.

From that moment on, I was a Duran Duran fan. Whenever he was around, I'd retreat to my room and blast their music as loud as I could—loud enough to be heard, loud enough to irritate, loud enough to remind him I was still there. I'd keep it up until someone told me to turn it down. It wasn't about the music anymore. It was about resistance. It was about reclaiming some small piece of control.

While I was rebelling against Wilmoth, David's rebellion was aimed elsewhere—at our father.

That summer, David agreed to go with Dad on what would become his last trip with him. We traveled across the country to pick up my sister Marina and her family, and then continued on to Disneyland. On the surface, it sounded like a family adventure. But underneath, everything was already frayed.

I remember one moment on that trip in particular. Dad, David, and I were play-fighting—roughhousing the way families sometimes do. In the middle of it, David hit Dad in the mouth. Hard. He made it look like an accident, but I knew better. I could feel the intent behind it. That wasn't play. That was anger finding an outlet.

After that cross-country trip, Dad and David only saw each other a handful of times. Eventually, Dad cut David off completely.

Looking back now—as a parent myself—I can say this without hesitation: my father's reaction to David was wrong. Whatever pain he felt, whatever hurt he carried, cutting off your child is never the answer. What began as fractured relationships became permanent breaks, not because they had to—but because the adults involved chose pride, punishment, and control over repair.

And once again, the consequences didn't land on the people making the choices. They landed on the kids caught in between.

People often talk about the story of the prodigal son, usually focusing on the moment when the son comes back to his father. But if you actually read the story in its entirety, there's a detail that matters far more than the return itself. When the son finally decides to come home, the father doesn't wait on the porch. He doesn't stand there with folded arms.

He *runs* to his son and meets him before the boy even sets foot on his land.

The father embraces him. He celebrates his return. Not once does he chastise him. Not once does he remind him how wrong he was for leaving. There is no humiliation, no punishment, no *"I told you so."* There is only love, relief, and restoration.

That story holds a lesson every parent needs to hear: your children are going to break your heart.

Mine certainly have. And I'm sure I've broken theirs at times as well. Parenting isn't about avoiding heartbreak—it's about choosing presence anyway. What matters is that every one of my children knows this without question: no matter what happens, no matter where life takes them, I am there for them. Always.

Unfortunately, not all parents understand the sacrifice and heartbreak that come with raising children. Some turn their backs when they feel hurt, disrespected, or rejected. And when that kind of abandonment goes unaddressed, it doesn't stop with one relationship—it echoes. It shapes families. It scars generations.

That's what happened with David and my father. They drifted apart, slowly at first, then permanently. And Wilmoth and I never grew together at all. Instead of healing what my father was doing to David—whether intentional or not—Wilmoth created a double standard. One child was compensated for distance; the other was treated like an inconvenience. I wasn't corrected. I was sidelined. I became, in his eyes, almost a nuisance.

Those dynamics don't resolve themselves with time. They calcify. And unless someone is willing to step forward—like the father in the parable—and choose humility over pride, reconciliation over punishment, the damage keeps spreading.

The prodigal son story isn't about rebellion. It's about response. And too many parents miss that entirely.

Nothing I ever did seemed good enough. At least, that's how it felt.

I remember my freshman year, when I wrote a history paper on **Ulysses S. Grant**. Grant has always been my favorite figure in history—not because he was perfect, but because his life was a story of profound redemption. He failed publicly. He was written off. And yet he rose again through grit, humility, and perseverance. Even now, every book I've written carries that same theme. Redemption isn't just something I admire—it's something I understand.

My history teacher, Mrs. Mayrose—still one of the best teachers I've ever had—gave that paper an A+. I remember going home proud, genuinely excited, and bragging about the grade. Instead of sharing in that pride, Wilmoth asked me why I didn't write about a Black historical figure.

To me, that question completely missed the point.

It wasn't about the color of Grant's skin—it was about the content of his character. It was about falling down, being counted out, and finding a way back. That was the story that spoke to me.

Another time, I earned a C+ in chemistry while pulling straight A's in nearly every other class. Around that same time, I was part of a small rock band in Brazil, Indiana. We had landed a gig—some girl's birthday party—and I was excited to play. Wilmoth forbade me from going. His reason? I should have done better in chemistry.

That punishment felt disproportionate and dismissive, especially given everything else I was doing right.

Now, I won't pretend I was an innocent teenager. I wasn't. Like I've said before, I didn't give him much reason to like me. I was defiant, stubborn, and increasingly withdrawn. But even so, the message I kept receiving was consistent: *you're still not enough.*

On weekends, when my mother tried to plan *"family events"* that included Wilmoth, I always found reasons to be elsewhere. First, I had my paper route. Then I picked up a weekend job at a radio station in Brazil. And when neither of those worked, I could always count on the McAfoos family to have something going on—some place where I felt welcome, wanted, and safe.

Slowly, almost imperceptibly, I became more and more alienated. Not just from Wilmoth, but from the family as a whole. Distance replaced dialogue. Absence replaced belonging. What began as avoidance hardened into separation.

And then it all came to a head when my grandfather died.

That moment would expose just how far apart we had drifted—and how much had been lost along the way.

I had just returned from Buffalo for spring break the week before when my father called and told me the news. My grandfather had died.

I was devastated.

As I've mentioned in earlier chapters, my grandfather played an instrumental role in my life. He was a constant: A refuge. A man whose presence gave me stability when so much else felt unpredictable. Losing him felt like losing an anchor.

I remember telling my mother and Wilmoth that my grandfather had passed away and that I *needed* to go back to **Buffalo** for the funeral. I needed to say goodbye. Wilmoth looked at me and told me I wasn't going.

I tried to explain. I told him I needed closure. His response was cold and final: *"You're going to have to find another way to say goodbye. You just got back from there."*

That exchange was the point of no return in our relationship.

As far as I'm concerned, he had no right—none whatsoever—to dictate how I mourned. Grief isn't something you schedule, ration, or deny. That moment crossed a line that could never be uncrossed.

A few weeks later, we went on an outing to a park to play basketball. I didn't want to go, but I went anyway. As we were playing, I thought Wilmoth had fouled me. Something inside me snapped. I completely lost control.

I need to be honest here. At fifteen years old, you should never disrespect an adult the way I did. I lashed out—physically and verbally. I screamed. I called him every name

I could think of. The rage that poured out of me was unlike anything I had ever felt. In that moment, I didn't care what trouble I got into. I didn't care how my mother felt. I didn't care how anyone saw me.

I had had enough.

I didn't feel like I was part of that family. I didn't feel safe, heard, or valued. After that incident, I didn't see Wilmoth much anymore. It wasn't that he officially left the family — my mother simply did an exceptional job of keeping us apart. I didn't want to see him, and it would have been completely understandable if he didn't want to see me either.

About eighteen months later, I packed everything I owned into my first car and moved back to Buffalo.

When I told my mother I was leaving, Wilmoth didn't wish me well. He didn't offer encouragement. Instead, he said my move back to Buffalo was *"suicide."*

Given the relationship we had, I don't know why I would have expected anything different.

What I *do* know is this: he was wrong.

I am proud to say that since then, I have helped raise nine beautiful children, built a decorated military career, earned my PhD, and written three best-selling books. My life did not end when I went back to Buffalo—it began again.

That chapter closed painfully, but it did not define me. And in the end, my survival—and my success—became the quiet, undeniable rebuttal to every word spoken over me in anger, dismissal, or doubt.

I want to be very clear about something: I am not saying that Wilmoth was a bad person. My mother loved him dearly, and my brother did too. Wilmoth and I simply got off on the wrong foot, and neither one of us was willing—or perhaps able—to change our steps once that pattern was set. On the other hand, my father did nothing to repair or strengthen his relationship with David. Earlier in this chapter, I talked about the chasm that was created during those years. All these decades later, that chasm still exists.

Ironically, my very first car was a 1983 Nissan 200SX. It still makes me shake my head how that year—1983—kept resurfacing in my life, as if it were a recurring marker I couldn't quite escape. I remember following my mother while driving down Interstate 70 on my way to the Indianapolis airport. My father didn't feel comfortable with me making that long drive alone, so he had my Uncle Douglas fly to Indianapolis. From there, we drove back to Buffalo together.

Before leaving Brazil, Indiana, I remember saying goodbye to David. What I didn't realize then was that it would be the last time David and I would ever live under the same roof. I also had no idea that the actions of Wilmoth and my father—and the reactions those actions caused between David and me—would ripple forward in ways that still exist today.

David and I have done the work to build bridges across that chasm. We have found ways to show up for each other when it truly matters. But the separation that was created didn't stop with us—it extended into the generations that followed. And the hard truth is this: it was the selfishness of two grown men that created that divide.

One of the most important lessons I took from this experience is how *not* to treat children who are navigating divorce or blended families. My first wife had a child after our divorce. She does not have a relationship with her biological father. Though she is not mine by blood, I treat her as if she were. I refuse to let her feel alienated the way I once did. I will not repeat that cycle.

I do not blame my mother. Not then. Not now. The responsibility lies squarely with my father and Wilmoth.

The greatest regret I carried from leaving Brazil, Indiana, didn't fully reveal itself until much later in life. It was the loss of a relationship with my younger brother. Today, David and I are both in our fifties, and I can say with confidence that we are there for each other when things truly go sideways. I will always remember how he showed up for me after the death of my daughter, Kayla, and I will forever be grateful for that.

But time has a way of shaping distance into permanence. Our lives ran on parallel tracks for so long that I don't realistically see us planning a fishing trip together — or even sitting down for Christmas dinner. That isn't bitterness. It's simply the truth.

If you are reading this as a parent — especially one navigating a broken or blended family — please take heed. The decisions you make in moments of anger, pride, or retaliation against your ex-spouse do not stop with you. They land on your children. And if left unchecked, they can echo through generations.

Both my father and Wilmoth have passed on. Yet the selfish decisions they made in the 1980s are still affecting people today — people who never even met them. That is the true cost of unresolved pride and misplaced loyalty.

And that is the lesson I hope never has to be relearned by the next generation.

Chapter 10

I Am Trunnis Goggins

It was the following Friday, and as promised, I went back to the hospital to visit my father. This time I brought my daughter, Mona, with me. My father was visibly excited to see her, as he had always been extremely close to my children. When he was healthy, he regularly came to my house and picked them up so they could spend portions of the summer with him in Niagara-on-the-Lake, Ontario. Mona's visit was special not only because she came to see her grandfather, but also because she was helping Janice at Skateland during skating sessions. With her involvement, Mona became the third generation of our family to work in that building.

When Mona and Janice left for Skateland, it was once again just my father and me. After expressing how proud he was of Mona and commenting on how much she had grown, he looked at me and said, *"Boy, you have always stuck by me."* I smiled and acknowledged the deep bond we shared as father and son. Internally, however, I knew that statement was not entirely accurate. Like any relationship, ours had its difficult moments, and some of those moments will be shared in future chapters. Despite everything, I did try to stay by my father's side as much as possible.

In the previous chapter, I mentioned moving back to Buffalo, but this return was different from the first time. Previously, my father and I lived alone together, but this time, Janice was part of the household. She was no longer just one of the women who *"took care of me"* during elementary school; she was now officially family. That family, however, did not immediately blend together smoothly. I remember overhearing an intense discussion between my father and Janice about whether I should be allowed to come back home. The following morning, my father sat me down and told me I had to convince Janice that I belonged there.

At that point, I felt like a *man without a country*. The phrase comes from a short story written in 1863 by Edward Everett Hale, which tells the story of a soldier condemned to live at sea for the rest of his life after being found guilty of treason. I remembered reading that story in high school social studies and feeling a deep connection to it in that moment. Like that soldier, I felt as though I had no true homeland. I am certain this feeling is not unique to my experience as a teenager. Divorce affects not only the spouses involved but also the children who are often caught in the emotional crossfire.

In their pursuit of a new life, parents can unintentionally alienate their children, leaving them feeling displaced or even *"homeless."* Navigating this kind of emotional terrain is incredibly difficult for a child, especially when they lack the language or emotional maturity to explain what they are feeling. In my case, I no longer felt that I belonged in Indiana, and when I returned to Buffalo, I found myself having to earn acceptance in the very home where I had grown up. That sense of not fully belonging anywhere leaves a lasting mark. This experience became a powerful lesson that I would later recognize in my own children as I attempted to blend a new family together.

Looking back now with greater self-awareness, I must admit that I was guilty of doing the very thing that once hurt me. In my effort to create stability and make a new family work, there were moments when my children felt sidelined, unheard, or emotionally displaced. They eventually shared with me that they had experienced many of the same feelings I once carried, and while I was grateful for their honesty, it forced me to confront my own blind spots as a parent. I often reflect on how much confusion and pain could have been avoided had I recognized those emotions earlier and addressed them directly.

This is why transparency is absolutely critical when building a blended family. Parents must be honest not only with their children, but also with their new partner, about fears, expectations, boundaries, and emotional realities. When communication is avoided or minimized, children are left to fill in the gaps on their own, often internalizing blame or developing unhealthy coping mechanisms. If these feelings are not acknowledged and worked through, they can follow children into adulthood, manifesting as toxic attachment styles, unhealthy relationships, and difficulty trusting others. Blended families can thrive, but only when honesty, patience, and intentional communication are treated not as optional, but as essential.

When families go through divorce, it is imperative to keep lines of communication open. There will be conversations that are uncomfortable and things that are difficult to hear, but they must be heard for healing to occur. Unfortunately, my father did not build his new family that included Janice and I, through gentle communication. I vividly remember him sitting Janiceand me down at the kitchen table and declaring, *"This is the family now. You do not have to like each other, but you will respect each other if you want to stay here."* What struck me most was that there was no room for debate. The more is that at the time at work. I remember using that same statement in one of my marriages, and that statement, along with other elements, led to one of my divorces.

I often refer to my father's leadership style, both at home and in his business, as his version of Pax Romana. Pax Romana was a period in Roman history marked by peace maintained through overwhelming power. Stability existed largely because rebellion was met with swift and absolute destruction. Similarly, my father established order through authority, not negotiation. If peace was desired, it had to be chosen, and that principle governed both his household and his business operations.

Despite his rigid leadership, my father did find ways for us to bond, and those moments stand out precisely because they were intentional. Every Tuesday afternoon after school was nonnegotiable family time with him and Janice. No excuses, no rescheduling—it was simply understood. Most weeks, we went to Sheridan Lanes Bowling Alley, where the sound of crashing pins mixed with awkward conversations and shared laughter, followed by a simple meal together. In those moments, the tension of our blended family softened just enough to allow connection to slip through. I genuinely enjoyed those afternoons, often more than I realized at the time. That rhythm of intentional togetherness left a lasting imprint on me, and years later, I carried that same practice into my own family, recognizing it as one of the few but powerful gifts my father gave me during that complicated season.

I moved back to Buffalo one month before my seventeenth birthday. Around that same time, Sting released his album *Nothing Like the Sun*. I had long been a fan of The Police, and his first solo album, *The Dream of the Blue Turtles*, had already opened my ears to jazz influences that still shape my musical taste today. For my birthday, my mother mailed me Sting's new cassette, and the moment it arrived, I put it straight into my car stereo. I began driving with no real destination in mind—just moving, processing, and trying to make sense of where I fit in the world. What I remember most vividly from that drive was hearing the song *"The Lazarus Heart"* for the very first time.

As the song played, one verse stopped me in my tracks and felt as though it was written directly into my life at that moment:

> *birds on the roof of my mother's house*
> *I've no stones that chase them away*
> *birds on the roof of my mother's house*
> *will sit on my own roof someday*
> *they fly at the window, they fly at the door*
> *where does she get the strength to fight them anymore*
> *she counts all her children as she shields against the rain*
> *lifts her eyes to the sky like a flower to the rain*

The lyrics immediately resonated with me, particularly the verse describing the birds on the roof of a mother's house. At the time, I had not spoken much with my mother since returning to Buffalo, yet in those few lines I suddenly *saw* her in a way I never had before. I began to imagine what she may have been enduring—trying to hold together a household filled with four strong-willed males, two grown men and two boys barreling toward manhood, all stubborn, all convinced they were right, and none particularly skilled at compromise. That realization landed with a quiet heaviness, the kind that makes you pull the car over and sit with your thoughts a little longer than planned.

With age and experience, I came to understand Sting's metaphor more deeply. The *"birds"* are the troubles that perch just outside our lives—financial pressures, emotional wounds, spiritual battles—constantly threatening to fly through our windows and doors. As parents, we exhaust ourselves trying to chase those birds away, shielding our children from storms they are not yet ready to face. Only later do we realize how much effort, sacrifice, and silent strength it took to keep us dry while standing in the rain themselves. Looking back, I realize how often we judge our parents without understanding what they protected us from. Many of their decisions were acts of sacrifice we only appreciate with maturity.

As I mentioned earlier, my father was remarkably lenient with me when I returned to Buffalo. I had responsibilities— working at Skateland was nonnegotiable—but Friday nights were mine, and I took full advantage of that freedom. My curfew was 2:00 a.m., which in my mind felt limitless. I had the run of Buffalo, Niagara Falls, and even the Niagara Peninsula in Ontario, Canada, and at seventeen, that kind of freedom felt intoxicating. My father owned a nightclub inside a skating rink, so I never had to look far for attention or company of a female. Years later, when one of my sons once asked my father what I was like as a teenager, his answer was simple and telling: *"Your dad had fun."*

Looking back now, I'm not sure *"fun"* is the right word. What I see more clearly is a pattern quietly repeating itself. As I was becoming a man, I was behaving much like my father had when I was a child—back when he cycled through two or three *"stepmothers"* a day and treated relationships as disposable. I never crossed the line into abuse, but I did lead women on, allowing them to believe they were the only one when they were not. Eventually, the teenagers in Buffalo bored me, and I began crossing the border into Canada, lying about my age and repeating the same behavior there. It was the late 1980s, and I can admit now that I was lucky I didn't walk away with consequences far more permanent than just memories. In those moments, I thought I was enjoying life, and my father was proud of the man he believed I was becoming—but in hindsight, I see a young man mistaking freedom for fulfillment and repetition for maturity.

Even at Skateland, my father was quietly grooming me to be the heir apparent. He didn't announce it outright; instead, he taught through exposure. He let me sit in on business meetings, observe how deals were made, and watch how relationships were cultivated long before contracts were signed. It was through him that I learned the true art of networking—not the shallow exchange of business cards, but the deeper understanding of influence, access, and timing.

Along the way, he also began educating me in something just as powerful and far more complicated: politics.

The year 1988 was an election year, and my father was invited to several high-profile political fundraisers. One of them was for Congressman Jack Kemp, a conservative Republican and one of the architects of supply-side economics. My father insisted that I attend with him, making it clear this was not optional but instructional. I remember him writing a check, shaking hands, and taking a photo with Kemp—also a former Buffalo Bills quarterback. In that moment, I remember thinking, *Wow, we're a Republican family.* It felt definitive, like a label had just been applied.

Not long after, we were invited to a fundraiser hosted by Mario Cuomo. While I don't believe it was tied directly to a campaign—he had been reelected Governor of New York in 1986—Cuomo could not have been more different from Kemp. He was a Democrat and considered quite liberal for his time. Yet there we were again: another check written, another handshake, another photograph, and then home. Confused, I finally asked my father why he supported two politicians with completely opposing ideologies.

His answer stuck with me: *this country is run by a different kind of people—Washingtons, Lincolns, Hamiltons, Jacksons, Grants, and Franklins—and as long as you have enough of those in your pocket, you have power.* I don't believe he was talking about bribery; he was talking about influence, access, and the undeniable role money plays in the political system. My father was deeply cynical about politics. I, on the other hand, like many young people, believed the rhetoric. I believed the speeches, the promises, and the idea that integrity alone determined outcomes—at least until life taught me otherwise.

Years later, after getting out of the United States Navy, I learned that lesson firsthand. While living in Indiana, a political candidate promised me a government job if I helped him get elected. Given my military and legal background, it seemed like a fair and logical exchange. I remember telling my wife at the time that this was a real opportunity for our future. I did help get him elected, and he did get me a job— but it was the most humiliating, dead-end position imaginable based on my qualifications. I lasted only four months. That experience, more than any lecture, permanently shaped my view of politics.

What troubles me most about politics today is how emotionally invested we become in candidates. Whether it's Obama, Biden, or Trump, we often cling so tightly to rhetoric that we're willing to turn our backs on lifelong friends. One truth I've learned the hard way is this: you can be successful regardless of who holds political office. Systems matter, but they are not destiny. It is how you operate within those systems—and how willing you are to work with people who think differently—that determines real progress. When we finally accept that *we* are the vehicle for success, we regain our power, strengthen our communities, and move closer to solving the issues that truly matter.

That's enough of my soapbox—back to the reason you bought this book. When I moved back to Buffalo, things felt right again. I felt *home* in a way that's hard to explain unless you've ever returned to a place that shaped you. Even now, living in Asheville, North Carolina—a place I truly love—Buffalo will always be home to me. It's stitched into who I am. During that time at Williamsville East High School, I met people who would go on to become lifelong friends, the kind of friendships that don't require constant maintenance to survive.

We don't talk as often as we should—life, responsibilities, and distance have a way of doing that—but there's an unspoken understanding that when it matters, we show up for each other. And we do. Whenever I'm back in Buffalo, those same friends appear at my book signings, pull up chairs at dinner tables, and raise a beer or two like no time has passed at all. That's Buffalo. As I've said before, it's the City of Good Neighbors—but more than that, it's a city of even better friends, and it never forgets its own.

Although my father openly admired my womanizing ways, there was one young woman I cared for who complicated that dynamic. Her name was Stephanie Molson, and in many ways, she stood apart from the rest. One time, my father drove Stephanie and me up to the cabin in Cuba, New York, just outside of Olean. It was a simple trip, but it remains a vivid memory—one of those rare moments that felt unforced and genuine. Even then, I could sense that Stephanie and I were in very different places in life. At seventeen, she was already living in her own apartment, working, and continuing her education, while I was still trying to figure out who I was pretending to be.

I genuinely tried to build a steady relationship with her, but the truth is, she had far more on the ball than an immature kid like me could offer at the time. She eventually moved on, got married, and built a wonderful life, complete with a son and a strong family. Through the connective power of Facebook, Stephanie and I have stayed in touch over the years, and seeing the life she created has always brought a quiet sense of respect and gratitude. Back then, though, I believed my so-called Playboy ways were something to be proud of. I was chasing attention, validation, and an image of masculinity I thought I was supposed to live up to.

As I mentioned in the previous chapter, pop culture played no small role in shaping that mindset. Shows like *Dallas* and music from artists like Wham! and Stevie Wonder normalized infidelity and excess in ways that felt glamorous rather than destructive. I hate to admit it, but my dating life was also heavily influenced by another 1980s icon—Dan

Fielding from *Night Court*. If you've never seen the show, the reruns are worth watching, even if some of the humor wouldn't survive today's standards. Dan, played by John Larroquette, was a womanizing lawyer who everyone claimed to despise, yet he always seemed to end up with the most beautiful women. That lifestyle fascinated me. More importantly, my father wanted that lifestyle for me as well.

Contrary to what Wilmoth once described, moving back to Buffalo was anything but *"suicide."* In fact, I fit in almost too well. I was living out a version of success my father admired and encouraged. Yet despite appearances, I was not destined to become the womanizing nightclub owner he envisioned. There was another plan unfolding beneath the surface, one I couldn't yet see or understand. That plan revealed itself in early 1989, and when it did, it would fundamentally alter both my future and my relationship with my father for years to come.

Chapter 11

I Am Trunnis Goggins, II

While sitting in the hospital with my dad over his last two and a half to three months of his life, we talked about many things. We spent a significant amount of time talking about the past, and I truly believe those conversations were therapeutic for him and helped him with reconciliation in ways he needed. We also talked a great deal about sports, particularly football, which was our shared passion. We both loved the Buffalo Bills, and that common interest gave us an easy way to connect during a very difficult season. Another topic that came up often was cars. My father loved cars, especially exotic ones, and that was clearly something I inherited from him.

One car my dad brought up frequently was my 1987 Pontiac Firebird, which remains one of my favorite cars to this day. It was black with a gray bottom and gray interior, with an orange stripe separating the two colors. The car had racing wheels and was an absolutely beautiful machine. My father warned me that the car was going to get me into trouble, and he was right—it did on more than one occasion. That Firebird represented my senior year in high school in many ways.

When it came to automobiles, I could not have asked for a better way to finish that chapter of my life.

My senior year of high school also brought a great deal of self-analysis and personal change. As I mentioned in the previous chapter, I had a lot of fun after moving back to Buffalo, and that experience allowed me to rediscover parts of myself I had not explored before. Looking back, I truly believe my father lived vicariously through me during that time, reliving opportunities he felt he had missed. My grandfather—my dad's father—was far stricter than my dad, particularly when it came to dating, and his tolerance was nowhere near the level my father showed me. Because of that, many of the freedoms my dad allowed were likely freedoms he had wished for when he was growing up. The only requirements my father placed on me were that I keep my grades above an 80 percent average and that I work at Skateland whenever I was needed, expectations I understood and met during that season of my life.

Driving around in a Pontiac Firebird certainly helped when it came to popularity. Whenever it was time to hang out with my friends, everyone wanted to ride with me, and the car became a kind of rolling invitation to be seen and noticed. It did not just turn heads—it opened doors. The Firebird also attracted attention from girls, and I was fully aware of the confidence that attention gave me at that age. One young woman in particular, however, changed my life in a way I did not expect. In hindsight, I can say that change was ultimately for the better, because she forced me to pause and examine the way I viewed relationships. Through her presence and influence, I began to realize that my behavior toward women was not always appropriate or respectful, and that realization marked the beginning of a much-needed shift in how I understood responsibility, connection, and respect.

I am not going to share her name. She went on to become extremely successful in life, and I did not consult her when it came to writing this book, out of respect for both her privacy and the passage of time. If she happens to pick this book up and read it, she will know exactly who I am talking about. I hope she also understands that I am writing these words more than thirty-five years after these events took place, with the perspective that only time and experience can provide. People grow, circumstances change, and even my understanding of what happened has evolved as I have matured. Still, the impact she had on me remains significant. She taught me a lesson that quietly shaped the man I would become, and that lesson will reveal its full meaning toward the end of this chapter.

When I met her, I wanted her to be the only one. I put an end to my multiple-date Fridays and chose instead to focus my attention and time solely on her. She wanted the same, and I remember those days as genuinely wonderful—simple moments filled with laughter, long conversations, and the kind of excitement that makes time feel suspended. Despite being only seventeen years old, I began planning a future with her in my mind, imagining what life might look like beyond high school. How many seventeen-year-old young men truly understand what they are planning when they picture a future with their girlfriend? Probably very few. Still, in that moment, it felt real, sincere, and deeply meaningful to me.

The idea of having a steady girlfriend was something my father struggled to understand. Whenever he asked me about other girls, I would tell him there was only one, and I meant it. In response, my father offered two warnings. First, he said he knew the girl's family well and believed that, sooner or later, I was going to get hurt. Second, he insisted that I should always have a backup plan when it came to relationships. To him, commitment without insurance was reckless, not romantic.

As he often did, my father framed his advice using football. He reminded me that while the Buffalo Bills had Jim Kelly as their starting quarterback, they also had a dependable backup in Frank Reich. If Jim Kelly could not perform, the team would not collapse because Frank Reich was ready to step in. My father told me I should remember that lesson when it came to women. The moment he said that, my mind snapped back to 1983, and a surge of anger and resentment washed over me. I rejected the idea of ever having a backup, not because I believed myself to be perfect—because I was far from it—but because the concept felt wrong. Especially with this girl, the notion of preparing for replacement undermined everything I believed commitment was supposed to mean.

While I rejected the idea of having a backup at the time, the concept of maintaining a prospect pool gradually became more acceptable to me. Once again, I leaned on sports analogies to justify my thinking. In baseball and hockey, organizations rely on farm teams and prospects—athletes who may never play for the big club but are carefully scouted, developed, and kept ready just in case. Some of these players never make the roster, yet they remain loosely connected to the organization, existing in a state of potential rather than commitment. Looking back now, I can see clearly that my behavior mirrored that exact structure. I may not have labeled it that way then, but I was operating as someone who always kept options in reserve.

With the benefit of hindsight, I now understand that the difference between a prospect pool and a backup quarterback is largely semantic. Both ideas are built on the assumption that the starting player is replaceable. Both exist to ensure that the game continues regardless of who is currently in the lineup. At the time, I convinced myself that there was a meaningful distinction between the two, but maturity has stripped away that illusion. I also recognize that my prospect pool mentality often emerged when I heard certain phrases or witnessed specific behaviors from my partner—moments that triggered insecurity or self-protection. That reaction, I believe, was influenced, at least in part, by the environment and examples I grew up around.

I am not blaming my mother or my father for this mindset. The responsibility is entirely mine. Once I had a prospect pool in place, I noticed that I worried far less about losing my partner, because I had already prepared myself emotionally for replacement. I have often said that never looking back can be a strength, but I have also learned that looking too far forward can cause you to miss the present entirely. As painful as it is to admit, this way of thinking did real damage to the family I later created. For that, I offer an honest and unqualified apology. This is not so much a lesson from my father as it is a lesson I learned on my own and feel compelled to share.

My father and I had major points of contention over this girl, and it would not be the last time we clashed over one of my relationships. At the core of our disagreement was a fundamental difference in how we viewed women. I treated women as human beings—people with thoughts, opinions, and autonomy—while my father viewed them as having less value than men, a belief he carried throughout his life. I could never accept that perspective, and it created a quiet but persistent rift between us that went far beyond any single relationship.

I valued women's intellect and conversation, and I never felt the need to monitor their whereabouts or exert control over them. To my father, that approach was not just foreign—it was unsettling. He often expressed his frustration by saying, *"Boy, you're not like your father,"* a statement he once made in front of my sister Marina. Without missing a beat, she responded with delight, *"Thank God he's not like you, Dad."* The moment was brief but revealing. While I was not like my father in totality, I can now admit that I did inherit some of his traits, and those inherited patterns quietly surfaced later in my adult relationships, sometimes in ways I did not immediately recognize or understand.

Like most seniors in high school, the future weighed heavily on my mind, pressing in with equal parts excitement and uncertainty. I watched my friends enroll in and get accepted to colleges all over the country, each acceptance letter opening a door to a different version of life. A neighbor across the street auditioned and was accepted to play violin in an orchestra in Europe, a reminder that the world extended far beyond the boundaries I had always known. I applied to and was accepted at Fredonia, a college about an hour and twenty minutes from home, and I wanted desperately to go. My father, however, was determined that I stay behind and run Skateland, believing that path was both practical and honorable.

Like many fathers, my dad dreamed of his child carrying on the family business. I understood that dream, but I also watched the toll that business took on him day after day. He was an extremely hard worker, yet Skateland and the Vermillion Room demanded constant attention and carried relentless stress. Seeing that reality made me question whether inheriting the business also meant inheriting a life I did not want. Meanwhile, I listened as my friends talked about new cities, new experiences, and opportunities that felt limitless. Deep down, I knew there was far more to life than Buffalo, New York.

When I finally presented those thoughts to my father, I was met not with encouragement, but with discouragement and even shame. He told me there were countless kids who would dream of being in my position, ready to take over a successful business, and he could not understand why I would hesitate. I was not refusing responsibility, nor was I rejecting his legacy. I simply wanted the chance to see what else was out there before committing my entire life to a path that felt predetermined. That fundamental difference in vision created yet another layer of strain between us.

That strain was compounded by the ongoing court battle involving my mother and my brother, David. My father wanted me to testify, believing my voice could influence the outcome, but I refused. I believed David had made his choice and that his decision deserved respect, regardless of how painful it was for the adults involved. I also did not want to further wound my mother by taking sides, so I chose what I thought was the least harmful position—neutrality. At the time, and even now, I believed it was not my fight to wage. One lesson I want to share clearly is this: parents navigating divorce or custody disputes should leave their children out of the conflict. The emotional cost to children far outweighs any temporary sense of victory for the parents.

In the middle of that court case, my father decided we should travel to Brazil, Indiana, to see my mother and David. It was the first time I had seen my mother in nearly two years, and I was genuinely happy to see her. For a brief and bittersweet moment, all four of us—my father, my mother, David, and me—were together under the same roof. The meeting was cordial, almost fragile in its calm, and I could see happiness on my father's face as if he believed reconciliation was possible. Now that I am older, I can say with certainty that my father loved my mother deeply; the tragedy was not a lack of love, but that he never learned how to express it in a healthy or sustaining way.

We went to a truck stop to have dinner, and for a brief moment, it felt almost like a family again. My dad sat next to my mom, and I sat beside David. My father was visibly happy—lighter than I had seen him in a long time. As far as the negotiations were concerned, I truly believe that my father thought progress had been made. At the very least, he believed an agreement had been reached and that he was on the path to restoring his relationship with his youngest son. After dinner, he dropped my mom and David back at the house, and then we began preparing for the drive home.

What I did not mention earlier—mostly for narrative effect—was that Janice was waiting for us back at the hotel where we were staying. Another detail I also left out initially was that my mom, my dad, David, and I had spent several uninterrupted hours together that day. When we returned to the hotel, and Janice realized how much time we had spent as a family, she was furious. She immediately began yelling at my dad. I remember him trying to explain that he had done what he needed to do to make the court proceedings easier, but it did not matter. The damage was already done.

Then came the moment that ended any chance of salvaging the situation. My dad started to say something to Janice, but instead of calling her by her name, he called her Jackie. Everything went silent. I remember the look on Janice's face—shock, rage, disbelief—all colliding at once. I also remember looking at my dad and giving him the universal *"dude, you fucked up"* look. For any guy reading this, you know exactly the look I mean—the one your buddy gives you when he knows you are about to get absolutely lit up. There was no recovering from it.

We left immediately and started the drive back home. For the next 534 miles in that 1980 Mercedes-Benz, you could have heard a pin drop. No radio. No conversation. Just silence. It took my father about a week and a half to repair that particular faux pas, but the damage extended far beyond that moment. Although my dad believed he had made a breakthrough with my mother regarding visitation, whatever progress he thought he had achieved quickly unraveled.

A few months later, my father gave up all legal rights to David. Around the same time, my relationship with both of my parents began to deteriorate as well, largely because of my continued *"neutral"* stance. In June of 1989, I graduated from high school. I remember feeling deeply disappointed that my mother did not attend my graduation, largely due to the ongoing court case and everything surrounding it. While I had a piece of paper that officially declared me an adult, I was emotionally weighed down by confusion—especially about how my mother and my brother felt about me.

With time and perspective, I now understand that my mother's absence had nothing to do with me personally. It had everything to do with the emotional and legal fallout of Family Court. At the time, however, that distinction was impossible to separate. Graduation should have marked a clean transition into adulthood, but instead, it became another moment shaped by unresolved conflict, unanswered questions, and the quiet realization that some family fractures do not heal on a neat timeline.

High school graduation brought with it a deep sense of uncertainty. That uncertainty quickly turned into tension between my father and me, especially as the relationship with the girl I mentioned earlier in this chapter continued to grow more serious. My refusal to find a *"backup,"* combined with my desire for independence, only added to my father's frustration. Since I did not have the financial means to attend Fredonia, I made the decision to get a full-time job instead. My first full-time position out of high school was at Moore Business Forms, a company that, as far as I know, was later taken over by 3M. The factory produced yellow *"Return to Sender"* labels for the United States Postal Service, and I worked there as a maintenance man.

It was a swing-shift position, and I will say without hesitation that the job was harder than Skateland ever was— not because of the work itself, but because of the schedule. Swing shift is brutal. It disrupts your sleep, your social life, and your sense of time altogether. To this day, whenever I meet someone who works swing shift, I feel an immediate sense of empathy and usually want to give them a hug. When I took that job, my father was furious. He made it clear that if I lived under his roof, I worked at Skateland exclusively.

Because I chose to pursue a different life, I was effectively banished from my home.

My first apartment lasted exactly two days. The rent was $175 a month, which at the time felt like a significant amount of money. I remember opening one of the kitchen cabinets and finding a rat inside. I called the landlord immediately, and he laughed, telling me that at least I now had a pet. I did not find that funny. I moved out two days later.

After that, I temporarily lived with my cousin Keyes until I could save enough money to find another place. Keyes has always been more like a big brother than a cousin, and to this day, I still look up to him. We often laugh and talk about the time I stayed with him, and I remain forever grateful that he opened his doors to me when I needed it most. Not long after, I moved into an apartment in the Gates Circle district of Buffalo. I loved that place—it had brick walls and hardwood floors and felt like the quintessential bachelor pad. Because I was one of the first among my friends to have my own apartment, it quickly became the main hangout spot. I have no shortage of stories from that time, but some of them are best left untold to protect the innocent.

This brings me back to my 1987 Pontiac Firebird. After I moved out of my dad's house, I could no longer afford the insurance or the car payment, and practicality finally overruled pride. I made the responsible decision to trade it in and ended up getting a fairly good deal on a 1984 Toyota Tercel. It was a significant downgrade in every possible way, but I remember driving to my girlfriend's house in that little car with a surprising sense of excitement. For the first time, it felt like I had done something genuinely adult—choosing responsibility over image.

It did not take long for reality to set in. Less than three weeks later, my dad was proven right when that same girlfriend broke my heart. She told me she thought it was best that we both experience new things. At the time, the pain felt overwhelming, but it became one of the most valuable lessons of my life—one I have carried with me ever since and later shared with my own children. Looking back, I am sure my father warned me because he had learned that lesson the hard way himself. It is a lesson, I have come to believe, that most people only truly understand after living through it.

After losing that relationship, I slipped back into old habits, though on a much smaller scale. My disposable income was nowhere near what it had been when I lived at home, which naturally limited my options. Not long after, I met a young woman named Sandy. I met her at a now-defunct nightclub in a mall called Club Exit in Niagara Falls, New York. Sandy lived in St. Catharines, Ontario, and I will never forget walking up to her, asking her to dance, and having her say yes.

We exchanged phone numbers and met again the very next day in a quieter, more relaxed setting. Sandy was a genuinely sweet young woman, and we connected almost instantly. From the start, there was an ease between us that felt different—less chaotic, more sincere. At that point in my life, that difference mattered more than I fully understood at the time.

For the first time in years, I decided to return to Brazil, Indiana, to spend the Thanksgiving holiday with my mother and my grandparents. Sandy and I were getting along so well that she decided to come with me, which felt significant at the time. It was one thing to visit family alone; it was another to bring someone new into that part of my past. In my brother David's book, he talks about the Ku Klux Klan marching in a parade in Brazil. Some people dispute that account. Personally, I was not there to witness any parade because I did not stay in Brazil very long during that period.

What I do know—without question—is that during that Thanksgiving weekend, when I brought Sandy, a white Canadian woman, to Brazil, Indiana, we encountered Klansmen standing on the corner of U.S. Highway 40 and State Road 59 selling Ku Klux Klan magazines. I will never forget the look of horror on Sandy's face. She told me she had only ever seen something like that in movies. Her disbelief made the moment even heavier, as if reality had abruptly shattered a sense of distance she once believed existed between hatred and everyday life.

In response, and perhaps driven by a mix of anger, defiance, and immaturity, I decided to be a troublemaker. I pulled over and walked up to them to buy one of their publications. Even though they were wearing their hoods, I remember the confusion in their body language when they saw me approach and hand over a dollar. It was a small, almost absurd interaction, but it reinforced something I had already learned and spoken about earlier in this book: racism exists everywhere. What ultimately determines its power is how people choose to respond to it.

That same Thanksgiving weekend also marked the last time I would ever sit down and have a conversation with Wilmoth. I remember him commenting on my current situation, telling me that I was working a dead-end job and needed to reconsider my life choices. I remember my response clearly, even if the exact words have faded with time. What has never faded is the sense of finality in that exchange. If I knew that that would be the last conversation we would ever have, I would've spoken differently.

Sandy and I returned to Brazil, Indiana, again for Christmas, and once more we spent time with my mother. Looking back, I think I was trying to make up for the years I had missed with her, attempting to reclaim time that could never truly be replaced. On the drive home, we were caught in a severe snowstorm. The snowfall was so heavy that authorities closed a section of Interstate 90 just after Erie, Pennsylvania, forcing us to find a hotel and spend the night. I remember calling home to let my family know we would not make it back as planned. Wilmoth answered the phone, and I passed along the message, unaware that it would never reach anyone else in my family.

A few days later, my grandmother called to tell me that Wilmoth had died. She explained that she had just returned from the funeral and wanted to notify me personally. His death came as a shock. He is the only person in my life who passed away with whom there was no resolution, no final conversation, and no chance to reconcile lingering differences. I know my mother and my brother were deeply hurt by his passing. When I heard the news, my first reaction was concern for David and my mom. As for my own emotions, I honestly did not know what I felt. Even now, I often wonder what my relationship with my mother might look like had Wilmoth still been alive. He was good to her, and he was good to my brother, and for that, I remain grateful for the role he played in their lives.

I will always view the 1980s as the decade that laid the foundation for who I became. The way I learned to handle heartache, disappointment, success, relationships, and even faith was shaped during those years. On New Year's Eve, I took Sandy and her brother to a Buffalo Sabres hockey game—they were playing the New York Islanders. After the game, as we drove back toward St. Catharines, Ontario, I turned on the radio. The announcer was recapping the major events of 1989, a year filled with historic change. One of the most significant moments mentioned was the fall of the Berlin Wall. As people in Eastern Europe experienced independence from communist rule for the first time, I realized I was experiencing a form of independence of my own.

Life as I had known it had changed completely. I was no longer living under the influence or authority of either my mother or my father. For the first time, I was navigating the world on my own terms. As I drove along the QEW that night, I smiled quietly to myself, believing—perhaps for the first time with real conviction—that brighter days were ahead.

Chapter 12

The Dark Ages: Freedom, Disorder, and a Personal Parallel

The Dark Ages in European history refer to a roughly five-hundred-year period that began after the fall of Rome in the late fifth century C.E. While modern historians use the term less frequently today, it still represents a prolonged era marked by instability, fragmentation, and uncertainty across much of Europe. Although there were meaningful advances in agriculture and technology during this time, the dominant narrative remains one of disorder, barbarism, and chaos. With the collapse of Roman authority, long-suppressed cultures were suddenly free to pursue their own destinies, yet many lacked the structure or experience to govern themselves effectively. Some societies descended into anarchy, others were conquered, and still others vanished entirely. Survival, rather than progress, became the primary concern.

Interestingly, even something as simple as the French fry traces part of its origin to this era. During the Dark Ages, the potato became an essential crop because it grew underground, protected from invading armies who burned fields and villages. Fire rarely reached deep enough to destroy the potatoes, allowing people to survive when other food sources were wiped out. In many ways, this quiet resilience beneath the surface mirrors periods of human struggle, when survival depends on what cannot be easily seen or taken. This historical reality provides an unexpected but powerful metaphor for my own life during the first years I lived on my own.

As previously mentioned, I moved out on my own shortly after high school and was no longer under the direct influence or rules of my father. I am quite confident that immediately after the fall of Rome, cultures that had been forcibly subjected to the Empire experienced a sense of euphoria—an intoxicating feeling of freedom that likely ushered in a brief season of optimism and relief. That is exactly what happened to me. Like those newly liberated societies, I reveled in my independence. I had what I considered the ultimate bachelor pad, a place where my friends constantly gathered to hang out, and escape responsibility. I held a decent job as a maintenance man with Moore Business Forms, earned steady income, and even had a companion for a short while. In that moment, life felt wide open, unstructured, and full of promise—yet, much like post-Roman Europe, the excitement of freedom masked the absence of direction and discipline that would soon reveal itself.

The summer of 1990 ushered in a season of sudden and sobering change. Sandy and I had shared many genuinely good moments together, but it became clear that our relationship was not meant to endure. As gracefully as we came together, we also went our separate ways. I have no idea what became of her, yet I truly hope she found joy beyond anything we ever imagined. Almost simultaneously, Moore Business Forms lost its contract with the United States Postal Service, a devastating blow that resulted in widespread layoffs, including mine, as the production of *"return to sender"* stickers abruptly came to an end. This moment forced me to grow up quickly. The carefree rhythm of independence was replaced by urgency, and my most pressing concern became securing another job so I could keep my apartment and maintain even a basic sense of stability.

In this case, the cloud truly did have a bright silver lining. I landed a job as a bank teller at Goldome Bank, right in the heart of downtown Buffalo. The position started as part-time, but I was always willing to fill in when other tellers needed time off, eagerly picking up extra shifts whenever they were available. One of the best parts of the job was the schedule— no swing shifts, no late nights, just dependable, predictable banker's hours. To further supplement my income, I also took a job delivering photo packages for Olan Mills Photography. That work ran Monday through Thursday evenings for four hours at a time, with every other Saturday morning added into the mix. Thankfully, I drove a Toyota Tercel with excellent gas mileage—because the thought of navigating

Western New York in a gas-guzzling Firebird would have killed my wallet.

I did miss Sandy. She was a genuinely good person, but instead of processing that loss in a healthy way, I plunged headfirst back into excessive dating. With my living situation now more stable, I became wilder than ever—if I'm being honest, probably downright disgusting. I had resigned myself to the belief that I would never have a family of my own, and as a result, I refused to become emotionally attached to any one woman. That said, I also refused to lie. I was always upfront about my intentions and clear that what I was offering was companionship, not commitment. Ironically, that honesty seemed to improve my dating life rather than limit it.

One day, my next-door neighbor commented on the steady parade of women coming in and out of my apartment. He rattled off the diversity—White women, Black women, Asian women, Hispanic women—and then asked, half-amused and half-bewildered, how I managed it. I fired back with a smart-ass response, telling him, *"Martin Luther King had a dream, and so do I—the only difference is, I don't think I need to share mine on the steps of the Lincoln Memorial."* He burst out laughing. Quite frankly, I think he was living vicariously through me. He had a wife, and from what I could tell, they were not particularly happy together. I often wonder whatever became of that couple.

Eventually, I was promoted to full-time teller, and for the first time, I was making what felt like really good money. I continued working my part-time job, and with the extra income, I treated myself to a 1987 Dodge Daytona—maroon on the outside with a matching maroon interior. That car became more than transportation; it was a symbol of progress, independence, and validation that I was finally doing something right. I started to feel genuinely good about myself. As time passed, my high school friends began moving on with their lives. They found careers, serious relationships, and new responsibilities. Some transferred colleges and left Buffalo altogether. We were all growing, just in different directions.

My circle of friends shifted as well. High school friendships slowly gave way to coworkers and people I met downtown, each group reflecting a new chapter of my life. The faces around me changed, the conversations changed, and so did my sense of identity. Even if I did not fully recognize it at the time, my life was clearly in transition.

One day at the bank, I was approached by a woman who worked as a modeling scout for the Merry-Go-Round clothing store. For those who don't remember it, Merry-Go-Round was the quintessential stop for teenagers and young adults— flashy, trendy, and convinced it was shaping the future of fashion one neon shirt at a time. She asked if I would be willing to model their clothes at a local fashion show, and she didn't have to ask me twice. Suddenly, I was making extra money, wearing free clothes, and getting regular haircuts, all of which did wonders for my already fragile sense of humility. I often joke that my head grew so big I nearly had to trade in my Dodge Daytona for a convertible just to fit inside it. Looking back now, I can smile at how invincible I felt, convinced life was finally lining up just the way it was supposed to—unaware that this, too, was only a temporary chapter and not the destination.

In the early 1990s, the Savings and Loan scandal swept across the country, and banks began struggling and closing left and right. The bank where I worked was hit hard. I remember one Friday walking into work and being met by FDIC officials accompanied by officers who had come to take control of the building. It was surreal—like watching the lights go out in slow motion. The bank's assets were eventually divided between two other Buffalo institutions, M&T Bank and KeyBank. For about four or five months afterward, I kept my job and convinced myself I was going to be okay. Then, as restructuring continued, I was laid off once again.

The timing could not have been worse. The early 1990s economy was weak, especially in Buffalo, and job opportunities were scarce. I had no college degree and limited work experience, which meant I was routinely losing out to more qualified candidates. Now, as a man in my mid-50s, I can look back and clearly see exactly what I should have done differently. Pride, however, was in the driver's seat back then. I refused to take jobs I believed were *"beneath me,"* and even though I knew I could return to work at Skateland, I flatly refused. Going back there felt like admitting defeat, and worse, it felt like giving my father a sense of satisfaction I was unwilling to hand over. I did receive a severance package from the bank, which was enough to cover my rent and food for about three months—but pride, unlike money, runs out far more quickly than you expect.

My Playboy lifestyle was officially over. Every single day, I went out searching for a job, chasing opportunities that seemed to disappear as quickly as they appeared. Even now, I wish I could sit down with my younger self and explain that there *was* a solution—that the chaos I was living in was not permanent. I often wonder what my life might have looked like had I made better decisions during that season. Today, I live by the 4Ps—purpose, planning, passion, and persistence—and I follow those principles with discipline precisely because I failed to live by them back then.

Like many societies during the Dark Ages, I was intoxicated by freedom but had no idea how to manage it. I had no real purpose. There is no honest argument that working a job, coming home, and blowing every dollar of disposable income partying qualifies as a purpose-driven life. I also had no plan. Once the structures I relied on collapsed, I had no contingency, no resources, and no credentials to pull myself out of the tailspin. Just as importantly, I lacked passion. I did not know who I was or what I truly wanted. I was so focused on proving that I was *not* , (my father), that I never took the time to discover who I actually was.

I loved showing off to my neighbors in the apartment building. I had cool cars, stylish clothes, and a steady stream of attractive women coming and going—but none of that reflected who I truly was. Quite frankly, it never did. It was simply who I thought I was supposed to be. When I talk about persistence today, I mean the ability to fight through adversity with intention and humility. Persistence is a beautiful quality; it builds strength and resilience over time. What I had back then, however, was not persistence—it was pride. Pride can keep you standing for a while, but eventually logic, reality, and practicality strip it away, leaving you face-to-face with the truth.

I clung to that lifestyle for as long as I possibly could—the beautiful bachelor pad on Gate Circle, the Dodge Daytona, the so-called *star* women, and the social circle that only seemed interested in you when you had money or opportunity to offer. When both of those ran out, so did they. It did not happen all at once, but it happened quickly enough. Before long, I could no longer afford my apartment and was forced to move out. I remember loading my furniture into a truck and driving it to my father's house, where it was carried down to the basement and stacked away like artifacts from a former life—evidence that I had once been someone I thought mattered.

My father did not allow me to stay. There was no shouting, no dramatic confrontation—just a quiet firmness that cut deeper than anger ever could. He told me I had to figure it out. One sentence he said to me that day has never left my spirit: *"As long as I'm alive, you will never go hungry—but you have to figure out the rest."* It was tough love in its rawest form, and at the time, it felt cruel. Looking back now, I understand it as one of the greatest acts of love he ever showed me. He refused to rescue me from becoming the man I needed to become.

Even then, my pride refused to release its grip. Although shelters were available, and although I had friends who would have taken me in without hesitation, I turned them all down. I told myself I was fine. I told myself I could handle it. In reality, I was terrified of being seen as weak. Instead, I slept in my car. For those familiar with Buffalo, I often parked at the Foot of Ferry, right where West Ferry Street comes to an end. During the day, people fished there, laughed, and gathered by the water, unaware that by nightfall it became my refuge. I slept there because the Buffalo Police Department patrolled the area regularly, and their presence offered a small but meaningful sense of safety.

Those nights were cold, quiet, and humbling. The silence gave me too much time to think—about who I had been, who I pretended to be, and who I had no idea how to become. This was the moment when survival replaced performance. The ego that once thrived on image, attention, and validation had nowhere to hide. This was my personal Dark Age—the collapse of a false empire built on pride instead of purpose. And although I did not realize it then, this season would become the soil from which resilience, humility, and eventually identity would grow.

Proverbs 22:6 in the Bible states, *"Train up a child in the way he should go, and when he is old he will not depart from it."* I can tell you without hesitation that this period of my life was no joke. It was anything but funny. I went from swimming in Rick James's pool—with a young Teena Marie looking on—and receiving a nickname from O.J. Simpson, to living out of a 1987 Dodge Daytona that was, quite frankly, on the verge of being repossessed. The contrast was staggering. For the first time in my life, I truly understood what food insecurity meant. I remember lingering around friends I knew smoked cigarettes, not for the conversation, but so I could bum a few before heading back to my car for the night.

With freedom comes responsibility, and with freedom also comes identity. It is imperative that you know who you are and understand your purpose. When you are secure in your identity and grounded in purpose, you are far more capable of building a foundation that allows your needs—not just your wants—to be met. The life I lived immediately after leaving high school was one of survival. And for a while, I was actually very good at surviving. What I did not know how to do, however, was thrive. That distinction would take years to fully understand.

Whenever I speak to young men and women today, I always bring up this chapter of my life. Although I eventually overcame this season, I now recognize it as largely unnecessary—an unwarranted detour caused by choosing pride over purpose. Survival kept me alive, but humility and direction were what ultimately showed me how to live.

Chapter 13

California Dreaming

I often tell people that the best time I ever had with my father was the last six weeks of his life. During that period, I saw a version of him I had not fully known before—more reflective, more open, and more present. Those weeks were filled with conversations that mattered, conversations that lingered long after the words were spoken. Like many fathers, my dad always pushed me to do better, and even when I reached milestones, he would remind me that I could still go further. In one of those conversations, he gave me what was likely the closest thing to an expression of pride I would ever receive from him. He looked at me and said, *"You made it, kid,"* and I smiled, knowing that was as good as it was going to get.

However, as you saw in the previous chapter, my *"road to success"* was filled with twists, turns, and unexpected detours. One of my earliest memories of being on my own takes me back to a late night on Interstate 190 in Buffalo. I was driving my friend Jason Amirian home after we had spent the day hanging out. It was one of those ordinary days that later reveals itself as anything but ordinary.

Jason had just bought UB40's re-released compilation *Labour of Love*, and at the time, the song *Red Red Wine* had surged back into popularity. The cassette played through my car radio as we talked, laughed, and passed the time. When I dropped him off at his house, he accidentally left the tape in my car—an oversight that turned into a small but meaningful moment in my life. Jason, if you're reading this, I still owe you that UB40 cassette.

As I drove back to my apartment alone, one song came on that I had never heard before. It was titled *"Many Rivers to Cross"*, originally recorded in 1969 by Jimmy Cliff, but UB40's version carried a smooth reggae rhythm and haunting harmony that immediately caught my attention. There was something about the blend of voices that felt heavy and reflective. Without warning, I began to feel emotional, as if the song had reached inside me and pulled something loose.

The lyrics felt uncannily personal, almost prophetic. It was as if the song was speaking directly to me, narrating both my present struggle and my uncertain future. It spoke of uncertainty, loss, persistence, and survival—of barely making it through life while clinging to pride as the last remaining lifeline. When the lyrics said, *"Many rivers to cross, and it's only my will that keeps me alive,"* I felt exposed. The line *"I've been licked, washed up for years, and I merely survive because of my pride"* captured exactly where I was at that moment in my life.

The song did not shy away from darker emotions either. It spoke openly about desperation, even touching on thoughts so heavy they border on the unthinkable, when it says there are moments of contemplating *"some dreadful crime."* But the line that truly stopped me in my tracks was, *"Oh, that loneliness won't leave me alone, it's such a drag to be on your own."* It was followed by the painful admission, *"My woman left me and she didn't say why—well, I guess I have to try."* In that moment, the song felt less like music and more like a mirror.

As I mentioned in the previous chapter, there were many nights when I slept in my car. One night, the weight of that reality became unbearable, and I knew I could not do it anymore. I needed a place to lay my head, somewhere that felt even remotely safe. Exhaustion has a way of stripping away pride, and that night, survival mattered more than appearances.

When my grandfather passed away in 1985, he willed his house to the entire family. His intention was simple and profound: no one in the family should ever be homeless. At the time, one of my cousins was staying in the house, and purely by chance, I ran into him on the street. When I told him about my situation, there was no hesitation—we went straight back to my grandfather's house.

For the first time in a long while, I felt comfortable. Once again, my grandfather was providing refuge for me, even in death. When I was a child, he had offered my brother David and me spiritual refuge by taking us to church. In many ways, my relationship with God was established through those early mornings and quiet rides to worship with him. That house was more than shelter; it was a reminder of faith, family, and foresight.

I believed that staying there would give me the opportunity to reset my life. My plan was simple: find a job, get a new apartment, and return to the bachelor lifestyle I had been living not long before. I wanted things to go back to how they were, to a version of life where I felt in control. But the pride still living inside me kept getting in the way of better decisions.

I wanted a job where I could wear a suit and tie, work bankers' hours, and keep my hands clean. I no longer wanted to do physical labor. Like so many young adults, I wanted success to come easily, without discomfort or sacrifice. What I had not yet learned was that life rarely works that way.

The truth is, you have to work hard, and often harder than you think is fair. The irony is that the things you work hardest for are the things you end up appreciating the most. At the time, when nothing seemed to be moving forward, I refused to look inward. Instead, I blamed the economy.

In fact, I blamed Mario Cuomo and the depressed economy of Western New York. Looking back now, I can say with clarity that the economy was not so depressed that success was impossible. I simply did not have what it took at that point in my life to dig deep and do what was necessary. Accountability had not yet become part of my vocabulary.

I also blamed my circumstances on living in my father's shadow. My father was, in many ways, the father of the east side of Buffalo. His popularity and presence made comparisons inevitable, and at that time, those comparisons worked against me. There was no real comparison to be made, but I carried that weight anyway.

As a result of all those issues—some very real, others imagined—I packed everything that would fit into my Dodge Daytona and headed back to Indiana. It was not a triumphant return, but a retreat disguised as regrouping. At the time, it felt like my only option, even though I had no clear idea of what came next.

I only went back to Indiana to regroup. The plan was never to stay long; it was simply a pause, a temporary stop before heading to wherever I truly wanted to be. The problem was, I did not actually know where that place was. I only knew one thing with certainty—it was not Indiana, and I had clearly worn out my welcome in Buffalo.

At one point, I convinced myself that Atlanta was the answer. In my mind, it represented opportunity, reinvention, and distance from everything that felt heavy. The irony is not lost on me now. At fifty-four years old, I live less than three hours from Atlanta, close enough to touch it, yet far enough to reflect on how little I understood my own direction back then.

Once again, I found myself in Indiana, still lacking the maturity and determination required to be successful. Geography had changed, but I had not. No new location could fix what I had not yet confronted within myself. Growth does not come from movement alone; it comes from accountability, something I was still learning the hard way.

Despite all of that, something meaningful did come out of those struggles. I met someone who was willing to cross a few rivers with me. Her name was Alicia. She entered my life during a season of uncertainty, when I had more questions than answers and far more hope than wisdom.

A quick programming note: over the next few chapters, you will hear the phrase, *"and I got married"* more than once. You can interpret that in one of two ways. Either I was determined and willing to keep trying until I got it right, or I was an idiot who simply did not have a clue. Honestly, both interpretations are probably true.

Either way you look at it, I have been married multiple times. I could blame my upbringing, my environment, or the examples I saw growing up, but the truth is much simpler. The decisions were mine. No one ever forced me to get married, and owning that reality is part of the growth that came much later in my life.

I can say without hesitation that Alicia was brave enough to walk through many of the same struggles I was facing. She did not simply observe them from a distance; she lived them alongside me. For that, I will always be grateful. There were moments when the weight of it all felt overwhelming, when the uncertainty and frustration seemed to pile up faster than we could manage.

One day, in the middle of that frustration, I remember looking at her and saying, almost out of desperation, *"Let's just move to California."* What surprised me most was not the thought itself, but the fact that she agreed. Looking back on the 1990s, there are many things I regret, but moving to California is not one of them. That single decision became a turning point, offering both distance from the past and space to imagine something new.

Alicia and I ended up living in Modesto, California, an agricultural town rooted in hard work and quiet perseverance. E. & J. Gallo Winery and Diamond Walnut were two of the largest employers in the area, shaping the rhythm of daily life. Modesto was close enough to San Francisco to feel exciting, and Alicia and I went there often, drawn to the energy, culture, and possibility of the city. We had a very nice apartment, and in keeping with my habit of remembering life through cars, we were driving a 1992 Chevrolet Cavalier Rally Sport.

For the first time in my entire life, I had a family. It was *my* family, one I was actively building rather than simply inheriting. It was the kind of family I had long imagined after watching the McAfoos family back in Brazil, Indiana. They had warmth, stability, and a sense of togetherness that always stayed with me. I wanted to create something like that for myself.

Not long after moving to Modesto, Alicia and I found out we were expecting our first child. In December 1995, our son was born, and in an effort to carry the name forward well into the twenty-first century, we named him Trunnis. I remember calling my dad back in Buffalo to share the news. He was at the Vermillion Room at the time and announced that everyone there would get a free drink to celebrate the birth of his grandson.

My sister Marina was living in Modesto then, and I remember her staying with Alicia and me at the hospital all day. She was there to welcome her nephew into the world, surrounding that moment with family and love. When I held Trunnis for the first time, I felt an overwhelming joy, but alongside it came an enormous sense of responsibility.

That moment changed me in a way nothing else ever had. For the first time in my adult life, I told myself that I had to step up. I had to dig deep. I understood that my life was no longer just my own—it was now tied to the future of someone who depended entirely on me.

For the first couple of months after Trunnis was born, life in Modesto, California, felt good—really good. There was a sense of newness, possibility, and hope that seemed to settle into our daily routine. I was comfortable there, grounded in the life we were beginning to build. Alicia, however, felt differently. She wanted to go back to Indiana, and that difference in desire created an enormous rift between us.

One of the biggest challenges I brought into my new family was my understanding of how a family should function. I had grown up in a household where the final decision was usually made by my father, and everyone else simply adjusted. That model was familiar to me, but familiarity does not make something healthy. Real families, I would later learn, are built on shared decision-making, compromise, and listening—things I struggled with at the time.

The divide between Alicia and me became unmistakable. She wanted to live closer to her parents, while I wanted as much distance from mine as possible. I loved life in California. I was developing my own traditions, creating my own experiences, and finally feeling like I was becoming my own person. At that point in my life, the smaller the dose of my parents, the better I felt. Alicia was the exact opposite.

The truth is, I was not listening. I was dug in, stubborn, and convinced that my position was the only reasonable one. Going back east was not an option, and in my mind, that decision was final. That certainty, however, did not last long. With the benefit of hindsight, I can say plainly that I handled that situation poorly.

I want to use this book to offer an apology—for my stubbornness and for not approaching that moment with greater humility. I could point to the model I was given growing up and say it was the only way I knew how to lead, but the truth is, I was an adult. I was twenty-five years old, and I knew better. If I could go back and speak to my younger self, I would tell him that there was a better solution—one that did not require digging in or drawing hard lines.

In true Trunnis Goggins II fashion, I slipped back into some old behaviors. Everyone has their vices. For some, it is alcohol, for others, recreational drugs, exercise, or extreme sports. In my younger years, my vice was women. It was less about connection and more about distraction, a way to outrun silence and avoid sitting with my own thoughts.

There is a song by Roxy Music called *"Love Is the Drug,"* and it tells the story of a man constantly chasing a *"buzz."* He drifts through red-light districts and singles bars, always searching for the next hit of validation, the next temporary high. Unfortunately, that song could have been written about me. This time, however, the chase felt different. Instead of excitement, I felt emptier than I ever had before.

That emptiness forced a hard truth to the surface. I knew I had to get back to my family, regardless of how broken or uncertain that family looked at the moment. I thought about the distance between Buffalo and Indianapolis and how deeply it had affected my own childhood. I did not want that pattern to continue into another generation. I did not want absence to become a family tradition.

There was also something else weighing heavily on me. Alicia was pregnant with our daughter, Kayla. The thought of her growing up without me being present in her life was devastating. Whatever mistakes I had made, I knew I could not make that one.

In 1997, I packed up my life once again, but this time the journey was far longer. It was no longer a 535-mile drive from Buffalo to Indianapolis. It was a 2,800-mile trek from California back to Indiana. I remember leaving Modesto and crying almost the entire drive to Sacramento, mourning not just what I was leaving behind, but what might have been.

It took a long time to stop replaying the *"what ifs"* in my head. I wondered who I might have become if Alicia and I had stayed in California. But growth often demands letting go of imagined futures so that responsibility can take root in the present. That drive marked another turning point—one paved with regret, resolve, and the fragile hope that it still was not too late.

When I returned to Indiana, Alicia, the kids, and I tried to rebuild a family. Earlier in this book, I said *never look back*, and this was a lesson I had to learn the hard way. Too much had happened between us by then. Life had moved forward while we were apart, and the experiences we endured shaped us differently. We had grown apart, not out of malice, but out of time, distance, and unresolved pain.

During our marriage, Alicia and I had one more child — Alexis. One thing I am deeply grateful for is that we stayed together long enough to bring three wonderful children into the world. I say this with honesty and humility: I am sure they all had to work through the consequences of our relationship, and perhaps even needed therapy because of it. Still, without hesitation, I know they were all gifts from God, blessings far greater than the circumstances that surrounded them.

As the years passed, life continued to unfold in ways I never could have anticipated. Today, Alicia and I work together to help raise our grandson, Jadden. Jadden is Kayla's son. As you know, Kayla — my daughter — was a victim of homicide on the streets of Indianapolis, a loss that forever reshaped our family and left a wound that time alone cannot heal.

Though Alicia and I now live very separate lives, we will always be bonded by our children and the love we share for them. Out of everything we endured, we found a way to work together—not as partners, but as parents and grandparents—committed to ensuring the success, stability, and future of the generations that come after us.

The lesson I want to leave you with in this chapter is not one I learned from my father, but it is one you need to know—especially if no one has told you yet. Before you begin a relationship with anyone, make sure your goals truly align. Attraction, chemistry, and good intentions are not enough to sustain a life together. Alignment is what carries a relationship when emotions fade, and real life sets in.

I have often admired how churches require premarital counseling, but I will be honest—I think much of it misses the mark. In many cases, especially with younger couples, premarital counseling becomes a formality rather than a filter. People who are in love and preparing to get married are wrapped in emotion and optimism. They are agreeable to almost anything because they are focused on reaching the moment when they get to say, *"I do."*

What I believe would matter far more is a serious, honest conversation about goals and aspirations. If Alicia and I had truly sat down and talked through what we wanted from life—where we wanted to live, how we defined family, how we handled conflict—we might have made very different decisions. More thoughtful decisions. More sustainable decisions. Love may open the door, but alignment determines whether you can stay in the room together.

When I married Alicia, I carried two very different sets of emotions with me. The first was elation—I was finally going to have a family of my own, something I had wanted for a long time. The second emotion was far less healthy. It was unresolved anger, rooted in feeling shortchanged by my childhood. Those two emotions existed side by side, and I did not understand at the time how dangerous that combination could be.

As I mentioned in the chapter about 1983, I should have gone to counseling years earlier. The unresolved feelings I carried from growing up quietly shaped my thought processes and decisions well into adulthood. Left unaddressed, they influenced how I loved, how I reacted, and how I handled responsibility. And while the pain affected me deeply, it did not stop with me—it spilled over onto Alicia and, ultimately, onto our children.

Chapter 14

Out of the Ashes

The year1998 found me living in a modest apartment on the north side of Indianapolis, navigating the unfamiliar terrain of fatherhood after divorce. Like so many fathers before and after me, I had my children every other weekend, trying to compress a week's worth of love, presence, and reassurance into forty-eight hours. Around that time, Sting released a song titled *"I Am So Happy I Can't Stop Crying,"* a haunting reflection on single fatherhood and emotional reconciliation after divorce. One lyric in particular—*"the park is full of Sunday fathers and melted ice cream"*—felt like it was written directly from my life. Every weekend, Castleton Square Mall seemed to fill with men just like me, pushing strollers, buying ice cream, and attempting to prove, both to ourselves and our children, that we were still fully present.

Even now, decades later, when I see single fathers spending weekends with their children, I instinctively understand the quiet urgency behind their smiles. They are trying to quantify and qualify their love in limited time. Years later, while playing beer-league hockey, I met a young father in the middle of a painful divorce. I reached out to encourage him, hoping my experience might ease his burden, but I knew from my own past that pain often drowns out wisdom. There is a reason psychiatrists compare divorce to death in terms of emotional trauma. From lived experience, I cannot dispute that comparison. My first divorce reopened emotional wounds from my parents' separation, and I was determined—almost obsessively—to spare my children the pain I had endured. Despite my best intentions, some damage is simply unavoidable.

While I was living in California, I earned my credentials in paralegal studies, and after relocating to Indiana, I secured a position at a large law firm. No, I was not a lawyer, but I genuinely enjoyed the work. There was a sense of structure and purpose in that environment that grounded me during a season when much of my personal life felt unsettled. It was during this time that I met a woman who lived in my apartment complex, and we connected almost instantly. Like me, she was navigating her own divorce, and that shared vulnerability created an emotional shortcut neither of us questioned at the time.

We married not long after meeting, propelled more by circumstance and unresolved pain than by wisdom. Looking back now, I can see clearly that there were many mistakes made in that relationship—mistakes rooted in haste, emotional fatigue, and a desire to rebuild something familiar as quickly as possible. Still, out of that imperfect union came three wonderful children, and for that reason alone, that chapter of my life will always matter. I could easily fill pages discussing the lessons learned from those missteps; however, this book is titled *Lessons from My Father*, not *Lessons from My Exes*, so those reflections will remain largely unspoken here.

During that same period, my relationship with my parents remained distant, even though my mother lived in the same city. When I reflect on that time, I realize that I intentionally created that distance, though I cannot point to a single, concrete reason why. Perhaps it was rebellion. Perhaps it was pride. More likely, it was my misguided determination to prove—to myself more than anyone else—that I could do life and family better than those who came before me.

Ironically, in trying to prove that I knew how to build a family that would last, I failed as well—and I failed faster. My parents remained together for fifteen years; my first marriage did not even come close to that mark. That realization stings more in hindsight than it did in the moment, because it forced me to confront an uncomfortable truth: good intentions alone are never enough to overcome unresolved wounds, emotional immaturity, and the weight of unexamined history.

As I grew older, serving alongside younger men and women in the United States Navy and later teaching as a college educator, I began to notice a recurring pattern. Many young adults create distance from their parents, driven by a deep desire to prove that there is a better way—*their* way.

They want to show that they can build a different life, avoid the mistakes they witnessed, and succeed on their own terms. The emotions I carried in my late twenties were not unique at all. In fact, they were remarkably common.

With the benefit of time, experience, and countless conversations with young adults, I now understand how predictable that season truly is. Independence often masquerades as wisdom, and pride can quietly disguise itself as growth. Yet what I want any young adult reading this book to understand is this: your parents carry more lessons than you realize. Their lives—both their successes and their failures—hold insight that no textbook, podcast, or motivational speech can fully replace.

If you have not called your parents in a while, pick up the phone and give them a call. You do not have to agree with everything they say, and you certainly do not have to adopt every belief they hold. But listen. There is a wealth of hard-earned knowledge available to you, a living resource shaped by experience, sacrifice, and survival—one that too many people fail to fully utilize until it is gone.

As far as my father was concerned, he absolutely loved my children. He came to Indiana often to pick them up, never treating the distance as an inconvenience but rather as the cost of love well worth paying. Even today, the stories my children share about their time with their grandfather are told with genuine warmth and unmistakable affection. Those memories are not casual recollections; they are keepsakes, held in their hearts with true endearment.

By this stage of his life, my father was living in Niagara-on-the-Lake, Ontario. He still owned Skateland, but he had made the decision to become a Canadian resident, trading familiarity for a quieter, more grounded life. Age, more than anything else, began to soften him. Sitting here now in my fifties as I write this book, I recognize that same shift happening within me. Things I once had little tolerance for no longer provoke the same reaction. My approach to life—and especially to my own children—has changed dramatically. This transformation does not happen overnight; it comes through time, humility, and lived experience. It was a journey my father was on as well.

What also changed during this period was my father's environment and, more importantly, the people surrounding him. The residents of Niagara-on-the-Lake were remarkably kind, and for perhaps the first time in his life, my father was accepted not for what he owned or controlled, but simply for who he was and the company he kept. He was no longer approached or treated the way he had been among the business-driven circles of Williamsville. There was no need to perform, impress, or dominate. For the first time in a long while, he did not feel out of place. He felt like he belonged.

When I visited him in Niagara-on-the-Lake, we spent hours on his boat, fishing and talking, often saying very little at all. Those days were easy, unhurried, and filled with a quiet joy that required no explanation. Looking back now, I realize that those moments were not just leisure—they were healing. They were proof that even a man shaped by ambition, conflict, and loss can soften, find peace, and finally come home to himself.

On one particular visit when my father came to pick up my children, he asked me to arrange a meeting with my mother. His request was simple but heavy with intention—he wanted to make one final attempt to establish a relationship with my brother David. At the time, David was away serving in the Navy, and although the odds were slim, my mother agreed to meet with him. That decision alone carried decades of history into a single afternoon.

To understand how that day unfolded, it helps to explain the logistics of how we exchanged the children. At the time, my three oldest children were still living with my ex-wife, Alicia, while my daughter Mona lived with me. For the exchange, Alicia would come to my house, and then all four children would leave together with my father. Alicia and my father shared a strong relationship—one built on mutual respect and genuine fondness. In truth, my father really liked Alicia, and their connection remained solid even after the marriage ended.

On the other hand, my father was not particularly fond of my then-current wife. It is important to say this clearly: she had never done anything to him to deserve that treatment. I believe the tension stemmed more from her background and from an early meeting my father had with her parents—an interaction that quietly reinforced a bias he was never able to overcome. As I mentioned in earlier chapters, my father had always felt out of place in East Amherst, New York. My wife at the time came from a background similar to those very circles, and my father often referred to her and her family as people who thought they were *"better than him."* There was no evidence to support that belief, but like all of us, my father carried biases that shaped how he interpreted the world and interacted with others.

That unresolved bias set the tone for their relationship and eventually became an obstacle—not just between them, but also within my marriage. What began as unspoken discomfort quietly evolved into strain that affected us all. Still, on the day my father arrived in Indianapolis, my ex-wife, my current wife, Janice, and all of my children gathered at my apartment. Without hesitation and without delay, my father quickly left with me and we went straight to my mother's home.

I will admit that the meeting between my parents was deeply uncomfortable for me. Although I was now an adult, far removed in years from the events of 1983, the emotional weight of that history rushed back almost immediately. Sitting on the edge of that moment, I felt like a child again — caught between two worlds, hoping for healing, and bracing myself for whatever might come next.

Here I was—now an adult, nearly twenty years removed from the events of 1983—yet the moment my father stepped into my mother's kitchen, those memories came rushing back with surprising force. Time may have passed, but the emotional residue had not faded. My father, arguably one of the most charming men you could ever meet, immediately leaned into that charm, laying it on thick as only he could. It was as if no years had passed at all, as though we had all been transported back into familiar roles we never consciously agreed to play again.

The three of us sat down together, and my mother offered my father a glass of scotch. If you have read *Stories of Transgression and Recovery*, you already know—and as I share openly in that book—that my father had a complicated and often destructive relationship with alcohol. I hesitate to label him an alcoholic, but there is no denying that alcohol was the culprit behind many of the problems that shaped his life and, by extension, ours. That day, my mother had purchased what was likely some of the finest scotch available in the state of Indiana, and my father enjoyed every sip.

There is a Latin phrase I first heard in the movie *Tombstone*, spoken by Val Kilmer in his portrayal of Doc Holliday: *in vino veritas*. Translated, it means, *"in wine, there is truth."* While scotch may not be made from grapes, I have long believed that it has an even faster way of loosening the truth. As the conversation unfolded, my father began to say things that exposed the deep regret he still carried over the dissolution of our family in 1983. His words were unguarded, raw, and revealing—truths that likely would have remained buried without the help of that amber liquid.

During the course of that meeting, I was still a smoker, and I vividly remember consuming an entire pack of cigarettes in less than four hours. Each cigarette felt like a small attempt to manage the anxiety and emotional weight pressing down on me. That afternoon was not just uncomfortable—it was emotionally exhausting, a collision of past and present that left its mark long after the conversation ended.

That meeting single-handedly changed the dynamics of our family. Did it reestablish a relationship between my brother David and my father? No. As far as I know, there was never any communication between the two after that day. However, what the meeting *did* accomplish was far more personal. It showed me that despite all the struggles I faced in trying to build a solid family, I was doing at least something right.

While my mother, father, and I sat together in my mother's apartment, Alicia, my then-current wife, and Janice were all back at my apartment with the children. Alicia and my wife at the time managed to coexist cordially, and I trusted them enough to sit together without my presence. That alone spoke volumes. Although I gave it little thought in the moment, I remember that my father had turned to my mother and said, *"Why can't we do what little Trunnis is doing with his family?"* In that statement, he acknowledged something he rarely admitted—that despite the turmoil divorce creates, Alicia, my wife at the time, and I had found a way to navigate our situation with civility, not for ourselves, but for the children.

As men, we all know that when former partners are together in the same space, anxiety naturally follows. I won't pretend that feeling wasn't present in me. Still, when it comes to my children, I have always been willing to shoulder discomfort if it meant protecting their sense of stability and connection. I would do whatever it took to ensure they maintained healthy relationships—not only with me, but with one another as well.

Another profound shift occurred during that meeting. When my mother left in 1983, my father made some harsh predictions. He claimed she would fail, that she would become a drug addict, possibly even a prostitute, and that she might not survive at all. I believe those words were influenced by his own past—his first wife had died tragically, and he seemed convinced that no one could live without him. Yet it took my mother less than ten years to prove him wrong. In the eight years following his declaration, her success didn't just refute his claims—it ran up the score.

When my mother left Buffalo, New York, in 1983, she did not have a college degree. I vividly remember that she carried little more than a glass Snoopy piggy bank containing just over $200 in silver dollars and Susan B. Anthony coins. By 1993, she had earned both a bachelor's and a master's degree and had risen into upper administration at DePauw University—one of the most prestigious institutions in Indiana. Vice President Dan Quayle was among its notable alumni, and while history remembers his misspelling of the word *"potato,"* he still reached one of the highest offices in the nation. If success were measured solely by spelling ability, many of us—including myself—would not occupy the roles we do today.

By the time of that meeting, my mother had accomplished extraordinary things, both personally and professionally. I am certain that her success weighed heavily on my father's ego. She had experienced domestic abuse, yet she refused to remain a victim. She chose progress over paralysis. Was her journey a straight line? No—but it was always moving forward.

As my father stood to leave, he reached out to hug her and said, *"I love you."* My mother did not recoil, nor did she embrace him. Instead, she extended her hand—a quiet but powerful gesture that spoke volumes. In that moment, my understanding of 1983 shifted forever. For the first time, I truly understood that healing does not come from dramatic gestures, but from small, consistent, forward-moving steps. No matter how heavy the past may be, it is imperative that we keep moving forward.

For those of you—both men and women—who have experienced domestic abuse in your lives, I encourage you to use my mother's example not only as a strategic model for success, but also as a living symbol of hope. Her story is proof that circumstances do not have to define destiny. My mother built a strong foundation through a support system that surrounded her with encouragement, accountability, and strength. She did not walk this road alone, and she never pretended that she could.

What ultimately propelled her forward, however, was not simply survival—it was her determination to thrive. She refused to let her past become her ceiling. Even the challenges she faced after my father were met with resilience and resolve, one obstacle at a time. Her progress was not fueled by bitterness or revenge, but by an unshakable commitment to move forward and build something better.

I would never claim to be the strongest person on the planet, but I can say this with confidence: I was raised by both a strong father and a strong mother. I carry the DNA of two people who endured, adapted, and overcame. Because of that inheritance, when I face trials and tribulations in my own life, I know—deep in my bones—that I possess the strength, resilience, and will to overcome whatever stands in my way.

Not long after that meeting, my mother's mother—whom I affectionately called *Morna*—suffered a devastating stroke. It happened on a day when I had taken her to her priest's funeral, a moment already heavy with emotion that would soon become unforgettable for entirely different reasons. She would pass away eleven months later, but even now, her presence in my life remains deeply personal. I was extremely close to her, bonded not just by blood, but by time, routine, and quiet moments of care.

Morna spent her summers living in Indianapolis, and she would often call me to her apartment to *"fix her TV"* or handle some other small, mundane task. I always went willingly, not because the task required skill, but because I knew there would be dinner waiting for me. Her beef stew—served faithfully over rice—was comfort in a bowl. And her bread pudding? It was, without exaggeration, the best anyone could ever make. The day before her stroke, she prepared one final dish of bread pudding, and she made it specifically for me. That detail still catches in my throat when I think about it.

When she suffered the stroke, my mother was out of town, and I could not reach my aunt. In that moment, I was suddenly tasked with making life-and-death decisions for my grandmother—decisions I was not emotionally prepared for, yet had no choice but to face. I relive those moments often, replaying the weight of responsibility and the silence that surrounded those hours. That experience marked me in ways words still struggle to fully capture.

The loss of my grandmother, coupled with the meeting between my mother and father, forced me to reevaluate how I approached family, connection, and presence. Tragedy has a way of stripping life down to what truly matters. That season of loss drew my mother and me closer—into a bond that remains strong to this day. It was during that time, in July of 2001, that I began calling my mother every single morning just to check on her. Those calls were born out of fear, love, and necessity, but they became tradition. To this day, they remain one of the most meaningful constants in my life.

During this same period, my professional purpose and direction began to shift as well. At the time, I was working for the Indiana Attorney General's Office while also serving in the United States Navy Reserve. Life already felt heavy, shaped by loss, responsibility, and reflection, when—just six weeks after my grandmother's stroke—the unthinkable happened.

On September 11, 2001, the worst attack on civilians in United States history unfolded before the eyes of the world. Like so many others, I watched the tragedy play out on television, unaware in that moment how deeply personal it would soon become. Amid the shock and disbelief, I later learned that one of my classmates from Williamsville East High School had perished in the World Trade Center. That realization turned a national catastrophe into an intimate loss.

To this day, he is still remembered and honored by our classmates—a reminder that history is not only written in headlines, but in the lives of ordinary people whose absence leaves a permanent mark. That moment, like so many during that season, quietly but decisively altered the course of my life, reinforcing the understanding that purpose is often forged not in comfort, but in crisis.

Christmas of 2001 brought yet another significant turning point in my life. As I mentioned earlier in this chapter, my father was never particularly fond of my then-current wife. Throughout this book, you have seen how he treated the women he *liked*—so it is not difficult to imagine the level of disrespect he showed toward those he did not. His approval was rarely quiet, and his disapproval was never subtle.

Over the years, however, I had developed a genuine fondness for Janice's mother, Janice's mom, who lived in London, Ontario—about four and a half hours from my home in Indianapolis. We visited her often, and she became someone I truly enjoyed spending time with. On one particular trip, I traveled there without my wife and was introduced to one of her mother's neighbors, who also lived in the apartment building. She was an attractive woman in her early thirties, but I gave the interaction little thought. I was married, had a family at home, and the meeting was insignificant to me. I returned to Indianapolis without a second thought.

What was insignificant to me, however, clearly was not insignificant to others. My father later learned that the neighbor had expressed interest in getting to know me better. Instead of doing the responsible thing—clearly stating that I was married—he worked diligently to arrange a second meeting. In his mind, replacing my current wife with someone from a different family would have been an improvement. It was a pattern I knew all too well.

He eventually invited me to London to spend Christmas of 2001. When he told me not to bring my wife, I refused. I made it clear that I would not spend Christmas without my family—and that my wife, regardless of his opinion, *was* my family. That boundary infuriated him. In response, my own anger surfaced—not only because of the immediate disrespect, but because this felt painfully familiar. My father had played a role in the destruction of my family as a child, and now he was far too comfortable interfering with the fragile family I had built as an adult.

The argument escalated quickly. I vividly remember him saying, *"Forget me as your father."* Without thinking—and instantly regretting it—I shot back, *"I'm thirty years old. I don't need a father."* The words left my mouth before my heart could stop them. Still, I am a Goggins, and backing down has never come easily to us. I did not apologize in that moment, and as a result, my father and I went eight long years without speaking a single word to one another.

What my father attempted to do to my family was wrong. There is no other way to say it. And while I wish we had handled that disagreement differently, the silence that followed became one of the most painful consequences of unresolved pride, wounded history, and words spoken in anger—words that once released cannot be taken back.

The lesson to be learned from this experience is simple, yet often ignored: do not insert yourself into the affairs of your adult children. With the number of children I have, I am certain that one day they will bring someone into our family whom I may not naturally connect with or fully understand. Still, that relationship will be *their* choice, and if I wish to maintain a meaningful relationship with my son or daughter, I must honor the decision they have made—even when it challenges my preferences or comfort.

Far too often, parents involve themselves in their adult children's lives in ways that cause more harm than good. In doing so, they unintentionally push their children toward repeating the very mistakes they themselves made at a younger age. Boundaries are not acts of rejection; they are acts of respect. When parents fail to recognize that distinction, they risk damaging relationships that may never fully recover.

I stood up for my wife at the time in front of my family, and I believe I was right to do so. Do I regret going nearly a decade without a relationship with my father? Absolutely. That loss still carries weight. However, there are moments in life when doing what is necessary comes at a painful cost. Scripture even speaks to this tension. In Ephesians 5, we are reminded that a son or daughter must cleave to their spouse and, in doing so, step away from the authority of their parents. In that moment, I acted in accordance with what I believed was right, choosing commitment over comfort. It was not an easy decision, but it was the one I needed to make at the time.

By 2002, my professional life was marked by structure, responsibility, and purpose. Being recalled to active duty to prepare wills and powers of attorney for sailors and Marines deploying to Afghanistan was sobering work, but it carried immense meaning. I was entrusted with helping young men and women prepare for the unknown, and in doing so, I felt useful in a way I never had before. Earning my first Navy and Marine Corps Achievement Medal during that recall only reinforced that feeling. Of all the recognitions I received in uniform, that medal remains the most significant—not because of rank or ceremony, but because it represented service beyond myself.

That sense of pride connected me back to my grandfather, my mother's father, who had served more than thirty years in the United States Air Force. I used to watch him attend church in his dress uniform long after retirement and wonder why he still wore it. After earning my medal, I finally understood. Service does not end when the uniform comes off; it becomes part of who you are. During the War on Terror, serving in the United States Navy gave me clarity, direction, and a sense of belonging that grounded me in ways few other things ever had.

On paper, everything looked strong. After a brief return to the Indiana Attorney General's Office, I was recalled again to assist with recruiting efforts. By May of 2003, my career was progressing, my responsibilities were increasing, and outwardly, I appeared to be thriving. Yet behind that professional momentum, my personal life was quietly coming apart. By then, my three older children were living with me and my wife at the time—a transition that brought both joy and an overwhelming new level of responsibility.

The same discipline and endurance that carried me through military service could not shield my marriage from strain. The weight of my job, combined with the demands of a growing household, began to expose cracks I had long tried to ignore. I told myself that perseverance would be enough, that if I just worked harder and stayed focused, everything else would fall into place. It did not. Instead, the distance between us grew, subtle at first, then undeniable.

I remember the moment with painful clarity. My wife said to me, *"My wish for you is that you find someone who makes you happy."* Under normal circumstances, those words would have sounded generous—even loving. But we were still married. I believed she was the person who was supposed to make me happy, just as I believed I was supposed to make her happy. She spoke those words on my thirty-third birthday in 2004, and in that moment, the contrast was impossible to ignore: professionally, I was building something solid and respected; personally, I was watching something fragile and deeply important begin to slip through my fingers.

A few weeks after that statement, we went our separate ways. This time, however, I wasn't broken the way I had been during my first divorce. There was no dramatic collapse, no uncontrollable grief. Instead, there was a quiet numbness—a familiarity with loss that dulled the edge of the pain. The band *The Police* has a song called *"Murder by Numbers,"* and one lyric has always resonated with me: *"Now if you have a taste for this experience... you'll find your conscience bothers you much less.*" There is an unsettling truth in that line. The more often you endure something painful, the less shocking it becomes. This separation was no different.

During my first divorce, I remember breaking down in tears over the sudden fracture of my family. That loss felt catastrophic. This time, the ending was almost procedural. I remember leaving for work on what would be my wife's final day in the townhome. I asked her, calmly and without emotion, what time she planned to have her things moved out. She gave me a time. I stayed late at the recruiting office that evening, deliberately ensuring that we would not cross paths again that day. The entire experience felt transactional—like closing out an account rather than closing a chapter of a marriage.

Although the marriage itself did not last, I will say this without hesitation: she is an outstanding mother. She has also been a good ex-wife and, remarkably, has maintained relationships with my children—even the ones who were not biologically hers. That commitment has played a significant role in keeping our blended family connected, and for that, I will always be grateful.

What struck me most during that season was the quiet irony of it all. Just seven years earlier, I was a single father who saw his three older children every other weekend. Now, because I lived in a strong school district and circumstances had shifted, those same children were living with me full-time. I did not view that responsibility as a burden. Instead, my mind went back to 1978—when it was just my father and me figuring life out together. If he could do it, I believed I could too.

One of the greatest lessons my father ever taught me was not spoken aloud. He taught it through action. He taught me how to be a father. And in the end, that lesson—more than any other—is the one that has stayed with me the longest and mattered the most.

Chapter 15

We Good?··· Yeah, We Good

This is the second chapter in which I start out by going through divorce—only this time, the stakes felt heavier because my life was fuller. I now had six kids (three sons and three daughters), and my three older children lived with me. On occasion, my first ex-wife's daughter would stay with us for extended periods of time. She did not have a good relationship with her biological father, and for most of her life I was the only father she knew. She has my last name, and although she's not biologically mine, I'm proud to call her my daughter. She recently had a baby, and the baby's name is very similar to mine—I felt honored by that gesture, and it reminded me that love leaves fingerprints you don't always see until later. She will always be a part of my family.

The *"bachelor life,"* which had been my default response after separations in the past, was now nonexistent. There were absolutely three reasons for this. The first was simple and unavoidable: I did not have the time. Between work and raising children, my days were already spoken for before they even started. The second reason was just as practical—telling potential dates that you are the father of six kids is, in many cases, an immediate nonstarter when it comes to securing a date. Some truths don't need explanation; they announce themselves and move on.

I remember one particular moment that drove this reality home. I had to go grocery shopping and had all six kids with me. It was summertime, and I was wearing Navy PT gear. I was in my early thirties and worked out quite a bit, so physically, I didn't look too bad. At the time, I was driving a 2001 Oldsmobile Silhouette Premier—one of the top-of-the-line minivans. I distinctly remember stating at one point in my life that I would *never* own a minivan, but if I was going to own one, it was going to be a good-looking one. It had dark-tinted windows in the back, which gave me the illusion—however brief—that my life wasn't fully on display.

As I got out of the car, a woman in the parking lot looked at me and said, *"Damn."* She said it in a way that made it clear she was impressed by what she saw. Then I opened the side door, and six young children poured out. That same woman said, "Damn," again—but this time the word carried surprise and something bordering on disgust. In that moment, I knew Playboy Trunnis was officially dead. Not wounded. Not fading. Dead and buried right there in a grocery store parking lot. And honestly, it didn't feel like a loss—it felt like clarity.

The third—and most important—reason I no longer lived the bachelor life was because I was now a man with daughters. As a father, I would have felt deeply uncomfortable living a life like that, knowing I had daughters watching me. They did not need to see that part of life at all. Even though I'm sure they saw more than I wanted them to, I did not want that version of manhood modeled by their own father. Some changes you make because circumstances force you to; others you make because your heart won't let you stay the same. For me, this was both.

Life was extremely hectic being a single father and a Navy recruiter. Tasks like getting three kids ready for school and onto the bus—one boy and two girls—were daily logistical challenges that felt more like military operations than morning routines. At the time, my daughters were in second and first grade, and my son was in third grade. I didn't know how to do my daughters' hair, and that reality became painfully obvious very quickly. That's when Kayla stepped up.

Not only did Kayla take on the responsibility of doing her own hair and her sister's hair, but she stepped up in many other ways as well—ways that no child should have to, but some children naturally do. When my other three children would come for the weekends, Kayla helped with them, too. She didn't complain; she adjusted. She became reliable, steady, and observant, the kind of presence that quietly holds a household together without ever asking for credit. Leadership doesn't always come with a title—sometimes it shows up with a hairbrush and a sense of duty.

Kayla was also a fierce protector of her little sister. One day, a neighborhood kid was picking on her younger sister, and Kayla was not going to tolerate it. She pushed the boy into a rosebush. Realizing trouble was likely coming, Kayla and Alexis ran back to the house, hoping speed might buy forgiveness. About twenty minutes later, the boy's mother showed up at my door with her crying son and explained what had happened.

I called Kayla and Alexis downstairs and listened to the full story. After hearing what really took place, I looked at the mother and said, *"This is on your son."* Kayla had acted out of protection, not cruelty. She had drawn a line, and she wasn't backing down. Kayla was always a protector. Unfortunately, as she got older, that same beautiful characteristic—her unwillingness to tolerate injustice or harm—would later become a source of her demise. But in those early years, it was simply who she was: loyal, brave, and unmovable when it came to the people she loved.

Though life was hectic during that time, when the kids and I get together now, we look back on those years with great fondness. My daughter Alexis always likes to point out that we ate cereal for dinner—a lot. It wasn't because we couldn't afford food; it was because I didn't like to cook. To be completely honest, the dinner menu at my house, Monday through Friday, was usually cereal, Chinese food, Fazoli's, or pizza. Saturday and Sunday mornings were different, though. On those mornings, I would cook—scrambled eggs, pancakes, bacon, things like that. But during the workweek, my life as a recruiter was time-consuming in itself, and coming home to cook simply wasn't part of the routine.

Eventually, through all of that chaos, I would meet wife number three. Once again, this is not a story about what happened during the marriage itself. However, it does connect to something I mentioned in a past chapter—how different elements can change the makeup of a substance entirely. This was another example of that truth playing out in real life. When you are blending families, communication and clearly established motives, rules, and outcomes are not optional; they are essential. I know that now at 50, but I did not know that at 27, and I certainly didn't know it at 34.

If you are reading this book and you are preparing to create a blended family, take the time to talk with your potential partner about everything. Talk about how you want your family to look. Talk about the rules you want in place. Most importantly, talk openly about how you feel about your kids. Silence in these conversations doesn't create peace—it creates assumptions, and assumptions almost always become conflict.

In my case, I ended up with nine children, while each of my wives had three. Because of that, when I made decisions about the children, I was always thinking about how those decisions would affect all nine of them. My wives and ex-wives, however, were naturally focused on how those same decisions would affect their three. Neither perspective was wrong, but the disconnect between them was real. In many cases, that difference in viewpoint became a direct route to ongoing problems. When everyone is counting different numbers, it's nearly impossible to agree on the final answer.

You can probably guess by now that my third wife also had three children. We got married during a time when things were going well for me professionally. I was doing well as a Navy recruiter—better than well, actually. I was named recruiter of the year for my command, and I later became recruiter-in-charge for my station, which was a rarity considering I accomplished it as a Petty Officer Second Class (E5). That kind of responsibility usually comes later, but timing, performance, and trust all aligned in that season of my life.

Although I've mentioned this in other books, I cannot thank Chief Petty Officer Buck Camfield enough. It was a single conversation I had with him that changed the trajectory of my life. That conversation pushed me to pursue my bachelor's degree, then my master's degree, and eventually my doctorate. I genuinely do not know where I would be today if it weren't for that moment. Some people enter your life for years; others step in briefly and permanently alter your direction.

My third child with my third ex-wife is Grace, and she was born with Down syndrome. She is a beautiful young lady, and it is because of her that I quit smoking. I will never forget the day she was born, or the list of medical issues that followed that moment. Shortly after her birth, she had to undergo open-heart surgery and spent a month in the hospital—a month that tested every ounce of patience, faith, and endurance I had. It was a very trying time, the kind that stretches days into weeks and forces you to measure life in heartbeats and updates from nurses.

Grace has been in and out of the hospital for multiple surgeries throughout her life, and I will admit that her recovery and strength are beyond reproach. She has faced challenges that would break many adults, yet she continues to move forward with quiet resilience. I am incredibly proud of her. If strength had a face in my life, it would look a lot like Grace.

Grace was born during a season when I was facing one of the most difficult decisions of my Navy career. If I stayed a hometown recruiter, I would eventually max out my rank—I only had one rank left to reach the ceiling in that role. If I chose to move, however, I could potentially advance all the way to Master Chief Petty Officer. That path came with a cost. It would have meant relocating my entire family and, more painfully, separating my children—my three oldest and my three youngest would move with me, while my three middle children would remain in Indiana.

Under no circumstances was I willing to put my children through that kind of division. I had lived the consequences of distance myself. As I've mentioned before, physical separation was one of the contributing factors to the fractured relationship I have with my brother, and I was not about to introduce that same variable into my children's lives. Ambition can be tempting, especially when it comes wrapped in titles and promotions, but I had learned that not every opportunity deserves a yes—especially when family is the price of admission.

By that time, I also owned a home in Indianapolis. It sat on one-third of an acre in a good neighborhood, the kind of place that finally felt stable after years of movement. The problem was timing. The year was 2008, and we were standing on the edge of the housing market collapse. Like so many Americans during that period, I found myself upside down on my mortgage. Stability, it turned out, was more fragile than it looked on paper.

The most pressing factor, though, was Grace. In her early years, she needed a team of doctors—specialists, my wife worked tirelessly to find and coordinate. If we moved, we would have had to start that entire process over again, and I wasn't willing to put her through that. Watching your child fight for health changes how you measure success. Career advancement begins to feel small when compared to continuity of care and peace of mind.

With one semester left to complete my master's degree, I made the decision to get out of the Navy. I've been out now for eighteen years, and I can tell you without hesitation—I still miss it. The Navy was more than a career filled with coworkers; it was a lifestyle built on brotherhood and shared sacrifice. Leaving it behind wasn't easy. The transition from military to civilian life was difficult, disorienting at times, and far more emotional than I expected. When you take off the uniform, you don't just change jobs—you redefine who you are.

Anytime you leave the military, the transition is difficult—most veterans would tell you the same. There isn't one single challenge that defines the experience for everyone, but there are common threads that show up again and again. Many veterans struggle with bouts of depression after leaving the service, and I will admit that I was one of them. There is a psychological shift that takes place, one that is hard to explain and even harder to overcome. You go from being part of a clearly defined mission to suddenly having to define yourself all over again. The uniform comes off, but the habits, expectations, and sense of identity don't disappear nearly as fast.

For a short time, I went back to working for the Indiana state government. In earlier chapters, I talked about never looking back when it comes to personal situations like relationships, and I learned that the same rule applies professionally. Almost immediately, I knew I didn't belong there. The environment felt familiar on the surface but foreign underneath, as if I were trying to step back into a life that no longer fit. During that same period, I was also working as an adjunct instructor for a couple of colleges in the Indiana area, testing the waters of a new path without fully realizing it.

Eventually, I accepted a full-time position at one of those colleges, and I would go on to spend more than eighteen years in higher education. Over time, the chaos of transition stabilized. Professionally, things were going well, and just as importantly, my personal life began to feel settled too. Stability doesn't always arrive with fireworks; sometimes it shows up quietly and asks if you're finally ready to stay.

I thoroughly enjoyed being a homeowner, and my kids loved the house just as much. They had friends, and because there were so many kids coming in and out, our home became the neighborhood "Kool-Aid house." Kids from all over the neighborhood would gather there, drawn in by noise, laughter, and the kind of freedom that only comes from feeling welcome. Almost every night, I found myself walking around the neighborhood, thinking about what I was going to do with the lawn or how I could make the place better. Our neighborhood was large, and those walks gave me space to think, decompress, and breathe. Yes, I was the typical suburban dad—and after everything that came before, I wore that role proudly.

Around this same time, Facebook was exploding in popularity, and for the first time ever, I created a social media account. What surprised me most was how many long-forgotten faces suddenly reappeared. People from Brazil, Indiana. People from Williamsville East High School. People from Skateland and the Vermillion Room. It felt like opening a time capsule I didn't know I still cared about. Catching up with all of those people was fun, nostalgic, and unexpectedly grounding.

Then one day, while scrolling through Facebook, someone who used to hang out in the Vermillion Room posted that my father had passed away. The rumor spread quickly and took on a life of its own. I remember seeing it and completely freaking out. The first thing that came to my mind was the last thing I had said to him eight years earlier. I sat in silence for a long time, staring at the screen, replaying words I couldn't take back. In that moment, regret felt louder than fear.

Surprisingly, the first person I thought to call wasn't one of my sisters—it was a cousin. I called her and asked if the post was true. Thankfully, it wasn't. I remember going home and immediately calling my father. Though stubborn will had kept me from calling him for eight years—and quite frankly, that same stubbornness had kept him from calling me—I knew the argument we'd had all those years ago wasn't worth losing my father forever. When he answered, the conversation started cold, cautious, and guarded, but it warmed up rather quickly. I truly believe both of us were relieved to be talking again.

We had been through a lot by that point, and I had grown significantly. My family had grown too. The last time I had spoken to him, I had five children; four more had been born since then. About a month later, fueled by the excitement of my kids, we drove to Buffalo to see him. It felt like we had never fought at all. Our relationship was reestablished, but this time on very different terms. He accepted the boundary that I was the leader of my family and that I would not allow anyone to jeopardize that. The irony, of course, was that I was more than capable of jeopardizing my own family without any outside help.

We did have some great times together after that. However, just like my second wife, my dad did not like my third wife. Trying to balance that relationship was exhausting. Both of them were incredibly strong-willed, and the constant tension stressed me the fuck out. That stress eventually led to the conversation that started this entire book in the first place. At the same time, my father was being diagnosed with what would eventually become a terminal illness. Because he didn't want my third wife around, I wasn't on great terms with him again, and once more, I missed out on extra time. Looking back now, I really wish I had handled that differently.

With all that being said, I did get to spend meaningful time with my father toward the end of his life. As I mentioned at the very beginning of this book, I am deeply grateful to Janice for honoring my father's wishes and calling me. It was more than an honor to spend the last few weeks of my father's life listening to what he had to say. Those conversations mattered. They didn't erase the past, but they softened it—and sometimes, that's enough.

In the first chapter, I talked about the time I had to take my father to the bathroom. While I was standing there with him—him sitting on the toilet, which is probably one of the most vulnerable places a person can ever be—I wasn't prepared for what came next. In that moment, he looked up at me and said, "Son, I need you to look at me." When I turned toward him, I saw a tear in his eye. That image is burned into my memory.

Then he said, *"Whatever I've done to you, I am sorry."* In that moment, I had a choice to make. I could have recited the list of things he did—and the things I believed he did. I could have used that moment to finally be right. But there was another option, one that didn't require proof or justification. There was the option of a blanket pardon. I chose the latter.

I looked at my father and said, *"I forgive you, and I apologize for the way I reacted and for the things I've done as well."* I only had one request: that he and I leave whatever had been between us behind us and allow it to stay in the past. There were no conditions attached and no follow-up arguments scheduled. And that's exactly where it remained for the rest of his life. Not because everything was forgotten, but because forgiveness finally mattered more than memory.

You may ask why I am sharing something this personal in this book. My answer is simple—although this story is unique in its details, it is painfully common in families. If you read this book for what it is, you'll find that there are many lessons woven throughout it. Looking back on my father's life and my own, there are countless moments where different choices could have led to less pain. If this book gives you anything, I hope it gives you the wisdom to recognize those moments sooner than I did and the courage to choose better when they arrive. Because in the end, we don't just inherit stories—we either repeat them, or we redeem them.

Chapter 16

The Reckoning

I cannot express how fortunate I was to be able to spend those last twelve weeks of my father's life with him. There are so many sons and daughters who are never granted the same opportunity, and I remain deeply aware of how rare and sacred that time truly was. During those final weeks, I witnessed a very different version of the man I had known my entire life. I saw a man reflecting on his journey with more regret than celebration, more introspection than bravado. Yet even in regret, there was honesty, and in honesty, there was humanity. Anyone who knew Trunnis Goggins Sr would tell you that he was successful despite extraordinary obstacles, an unforgiving cultural climate, and circumstances that could have broken a lesser man. He never allowed those factors to become excuses, and that same relentless determination lives on in each of his children.

I often think of my father when I watch Star Wars: Return of the Jedi, the third installment in the original *Star Wars* trilogy. For more than six hours across those three films, Darth Vader is unmistakably the villain—feared, hated, and remembered as the embodiment of destruction. He terrorizes the galaxy, enforces tyranny, and leaves devastation in his wake. Then, in the final fifteen minutes of his life, everything changes. In one decisive act, he becomes the hero who saves the galaxy.

The tragedy of that redemption is that only one person lived to truly witness it: Luke Skywalker. Luke saw the good in his father, but that goodness only revealed itself while Luke was present. When the moment passed, Luke alone was left to carry the truth of who his father became at the end. He was then tasked—quietly and impossibly—with telling the galaxy that Darth Vader was not only the monster they remembered, but also a man capable of redemption. Though his final act of heroism ended the war, it was also his last living act.

Everyone else remembered Darth Vader as the man who fucked up the galaxy in the first place. They never saw the sacrifice. They never saw the change. They never heard the apology, the repentance, or the quiet humanity that emerged at the very end. Unfortunately, that is the best example I can provide—and it mirrors my father's story more closely than I ever wish it did.

Every weekend, without fail, I made the drive to see my father. Mona came with me every time, and toward the very end, Alexis and Kayla—and sometimes Trunnis III—joined us as well. Those visits became sacred routines, anchored by consistency and love rather than obligation. Whenever my children entered his hospital room, my father immediately shifted into entertainer mode. He went out of his way to make them laugh, often leaning into self-deprecating humor that my kids absolutely loved.

He asked them about school, what they were learning, and what they planned to do over the summer, as if the future still stretched endlessly in front of him. In those moments, illness took a back seat to connection. On one particular visit, my father slightly overstepped his bounds once again—but this time, I let it go. He told my son Trunnis that he wanted to give him his 2005 Jeep Grand Cherokee Limited.

I thought it was far too much car for him, and I was ready to shut the idea down. But my father, never one to miss a teaching moment or a jab, reminded me—right in front of my son—about the 1987 Pontiac Firebird he had given me. I had no comeback. As I had already admitted, that car did get me into some trouble. Still, in that exchange, I realized something: this wasn't about a vehicle. It was about legacy, generosity, and a grandfather's desire to pass something tangible—and meaningful—down to the next generation.

There was one time we went to the hospital after my father experienced a medical episode severe enough to require admission to the ICU. Doctors had placed a tube down his throat to help him breathe, and they restrained his hands to the bed so he would not panic and attempt to remove it. The scene was unsettling—machines humming, lights harsh, and the undeniable weight of how fragile he suddenly was. Despite all of that, my father was still very much himself.

He gestured to me as best he could, signaling for me to come closer to the bed. When I leaned in, he motioned again, this time clearly asking me to remove the tube from his throat. I told him I couldn't. The look he gave me spoke volumes. Without a single word, his eyes said, *"Oh, if I could pull this thing out myself, I'd turn around and stick it right up your ass."* Even restrained, even silenced, his sarcasm and stubborn independence were fully intact.

Before his ICU stay, dad and I talked a great deal about his father. Those conversations answered many lingering questions I had about my own father's personality and temperament. As I mentioned earlier in this book, my grandfather was profoundly influential in my life, and he mattered deeply to my father as well. However, the man my grandfather was to me was not the same man he was to my father. He was not always the kind, gentle figure who picked up kids on the east side of Buffalo and took them to church. As my father described him, my grandfather was rough — extremely rough.

He was so abusive, in fact, that even as tough as my father was, he never liked dark places. The beatings my brother and I endured at my father's hands pale in comparison to what my father suffered as a child. That context does not excuse anything, but it does explain a great deal. Just as my mother provided a veil through which my father and I were able to bond, my father provided a similar veil that allowed my grandfather and me to connect in a very different way.

Like my brother and me, my father and I ultimately took two entirely different paths—paths shaped largely by our respective relationships with the patriarch of the Goggins family. Trauma does not travel in straight lines; it bends, fragments, and reshapes itself as it passes from one generation to the next. Understanding that helped me see my father not just as a man who failed in certain ways, but as one who was shaped—sometimes brutally—long before I ever entered the picture.

I remember one moment clearly. Janice was looking at my father as he lay in pain, very close to death. With quiet sincerity, she asked him, *"Are you scared?"* His reply surprised me. He said, simply and plainly, *"Yes."* In my forty-two years on this planet, I had never seen or heard my father admit fear. Not once. That single word carried more weight than any speech he could have given. I truly believe he was afraid of what awaited him when he closed his eyes for the last time.

That fear, I think, traces back to my grandfather. My grandfather showed *me* an example of a loving God. The God I was introduced to was full of grace—one who fed people, hugged them, embraced them, and reached out to the community with genuine love. Faith, as I learned it, was relational and restorative. It was something that drew people in rather than pushed them away.

The God my grandfather showed my father, however, was very different. To him, God was presented as vengeance, discipline, and punishment. While the truth is that God is a balance of justice and grace, when all someone is shown is consequence without compassion, there is a very strong chance they will reject the concept of God the moment they are able to think for themselves. My father did exactly that. He was not a religious man in the least. We attended church occasionally, but only when my grandfather was still alive.

There is a powerful lesson in that reality. Many people do not reject God—they reject the version of God they were introduced to. Today, when I turn on the television, I see far too many preachers talking about money, spectacle, and so-called miracles—not to lead people to God, but to lead money to themselves. That mixture of greed and superstition drives far more people away from faith than it ever brings closer. As a result, when the end draws near, many people are afraid— just like my father was afraid.

After my father was released from the ICU, doctors determined there was nothing more they could do. He was placed in hospice. That decision was made while I was still in Indianapolis, and I remember Janice calling me to share the news. I was sitting in the family room with the kids nearby when the phone rang. It was a short call—there were other things she needed to take care of—but it carried the weight of finality. I didn't think the kids were paying attention as I hung up the phone, but a single tear slipped down my cheek.

Kayla, one of the most observant people I have ever known—though, truthfully, she was also incredibly nosy—noticed immediately. I'm fairly certain it was the first time she had ever seen her dad cry. She looked at me, walked over, and said, simply, *"I love you, Dad."* I looked back at her and said, *"I love you too."* She said nothing after that. She didn't need to. In that moment, words would have only gotten in the way.

It was the week of Halloween, which fell on a Friday that year. That evening, I took my younger sons, Nick and Zach, trick-or-treating, while Kayla helped keep the chaos under control. All the while, I knew that once the costumes were put away and the candy sorted, we would be heading back to Buffalo to see my father. As we walked through the neighborhood, Janice called again. For a brief, terrifying moment, I thought I was too late—that he had already passed. Thankfully, that was not the case.

My father simply wanted to make sure I was coming. Because of the tube he had in his throat the week before, his voice was hoarse and weak, barely recognizable. He asked me if I was on my way. I told him yes. Like a little child seeking reassurance, he responded with a soft, hopeful, *"Yea."* I felt the tears come again. I remembered reacting the same way as a kid when he would come to get me. The roles had reversed—but only temporarily.

Early the very next morning, Trunnis, Kayla, Alexis, Mona, and I piled into the car and drove to Buffalo. When we arrived, my two uncles were already there. I remember my uncle Douglas pulling me aside and telling me that my father was waiting for me and genuinely looking forward to seeing me. Then, with a heaviness in his voice, he added, *"I don't know if he's going to make it."* That sentence hung in the air long after he finished speaking.

When I entered the room, I immediately heard what's known as the *"death rattle."* It's the sound of labored breathing from someone who is very close to dying—a harsh, uneven noise that fills the room whether you want it to or not. When my father heard my voice, he woke up. He looked at me and asked if I could get him some apple juice. I laughed softly, because for most of my life, *"apple juice"* had been his nickname for Scotch. This time, though, he meant actual apple juice.

I went to the small kitchen on the hospice floor, poured a cup, and brought it back to him. I held it so he could drink. He told me how glad he was that we were there and how happy he was to see his grandchildren again. Just like always, he asked them how school was going and what they planned to do over the summer, clinging to normal conversation as if it could momentarily hold death at bay.

Then he motioned for me to come closer to the bed. *"I have something to ask you,"* he said, *"and you can't say no."* At that point, I braced myself for some serious end-of-life request. I leaned in and said, *"What is it, Dad?"* Without hesitation, he replied, *"Get me out of here."*

I had just promised him I wouldn't say no, so I paused for a moment and chose my words carefully. *"Dad,"* I said, *"there's a wheelchair on the other side of that door. If you can get up and make it to that wheelchair, I'll take you wherever you want to go."* He rolled his eyes at me. I smiled and added, *"I didn't say no."* He looked at me and said, *"Well, I guess I didn't raise a dummy."* Even at the edge of life, he was still my father—sharp, stubborn, and perfectly himself.

A short time later, Janice came into the room, and we were all sitting quietly around my father's bed. He slowly looked around, his eyes moving from my children, to Janice, taking each of them in as if he were committing the moment to memory. Then he saw me. He motioned for me to come back to the bed.

When I leaned in, he told me to get as close as I could. In a whisper meant only for me, he said, *"You are living the life I always wanted to live."* As I shared in an earlier chapter, my father never told me he was proud of me—not once. But in that single sentence, he said far more than those three words ever could have conveyed. It was the most meaningful thing he ever said to me, a quiet confession wrapped in both admiration and regret.

I looked at him and replied, *"Thank you for making it so. I love you."* He answered, *"I love you too."* A short time later, he drifted off to sleep. In that moment, there was nothing left to say. Everything that mattered had already been spoken.

I returned the next morning. Janice took the kids to Skateland to help run the skating sessions, while I stayed behind with my dad. I sat beside him the entire day. He never got up. He never said a word. All day long, I listened to his labored breathing, silently worrying that it would stop while I was sitting there. It didn't—but the tension of waiting made every minute feel impossibly long.

Instead of leaving Sunday night like I usually did, I decided to stay one more night. Deep down, I knew I was never going to see him again. That Monday afternoon, I finally said goodbye to him for the last time. I'm certain he heard me as I thanked him for everything he had done for me. I told him he had been an outstanding father in spite of everything—that he had raised a man who took care of his kids. In fact, he raised six people who went on to be influential in their own ways. That mattered to him, and it mattered to me.

My father always had one rule: *Call me as soon as you get home. I can't go to sleep until you do.* I remember getting home that night around 2:30 a.m. I called Janice and told her I was home and asked her to let my dad know. At 4:48 a.m. on November 5, 2013, Janice called me back to tell me that my father had passed away. As loud as my father was in life, his death was silent. He simply stopped breathing—and everything went quiet.

I never went to sleep that night, or rather that morning. I went straight into my usual workout routine, then woke my kids up for school. I told them their grandfather had passed away. After that, I got ready for work. If you remember earlier in this book, that's exactly what my father did when his mother died and when his father died. Without realizing it, I carried on the tradition.

That following Friday, I packed the family into the van, and all of us drove back to Buffalo for his funeral. That Sunday, we held my father's wake. We had prepared a jazz CD to play in the background, something smooth and fitting for the occasion. Then we learned that the radio station WBLK was dedicating three full hours of airtime to my father. The DJ responsible for the tribute was Stoney Williams. Anyone who ever spent time at the Vermillion Room knows Stoney was probably the best DJ who ever spun records there. He wanted to honor my father the only way that made sense—through music, volume, and presence.

So instead of playing the CD we had prepared, we piped the WBLK broadcast through the PA system at Amigone Funeral Home. I'm not exaggerating when I say Stoney turned that funeral home into Skateland and the Vermillion Room all over again. It was loud. It was festive. It was alive. I had never been to a wake that felt like that in my life. At one point, I was almost tempted to go work the door, just to make sure the right people were getting in.

While I was standing by my father's casket, an older woman walked up and introduced herself as someone who used to date my dad. That part wasn't shocking—everybody dated my dad. But when she gave me her name, I froze. She was the woman my father once told me had tried to run my mother and me over with a car when I was two months old. I briefly considered asking her whether she took the bus or drove herself to the wake. Her answer would have determined how I exited that building. I chose not to ask.

Instead, she asked me for my email address. I gave it to her, and later she shared photos and stories from my father's younger days. I still have those pictures, and I genuinely appreciate them. That woman has since passed away, and I'll admit—I cross the street in Buffalo now with a little more confidence than I did before her passing.

In addition to all the people from Skateland and the Vermillion Room, my family was there. My sisters were present, along with their husbands, and of course, my children were there as well. My nieces and nephews were not, nor was David. At one point, we took a photo with everyone who had gathered. Given how rarely we all come together, that picture may very well be the last one ever taken with all of my sisters in the same frame. That realization didn't hit me right away, but it settled in later with quiet finality.

The funeral the next day was much quieter, much more somber. In that stillness, I reflected on the sheer number of lives my father had touched. When the doors opened at Skateland or the Vermillion Room, there were certain people you could almost guarantee would be there—people like Gary and Anthony Lane, and Landon Brown. My very first friend, Earl Foxworth, who has since passed away, came to mind. So did my dear friend Faith "Peanut" Patterson, who is still an avid skater to this day. She went on to become an entrepreneur and continues to live in Buffalo, and I'm grateful that we still stay in touch from time to time on Facebook.

My father was a major influence on the east side of Buffalo. In many ways, he was a father to people who didn't have one—or who needed another. I remember people coming into

Skateland or the Vermillion Room not just to skate or dance, but to talk. *"Go up to get down"* was the slogan of the Vermillion Room, but it became something more than that. People asked my father for advice about buying a house, making major life decisions, getting married, or even whether they should stay in Buffalo or leave. They valued his opinion. They trusted his counsel. He carried that responsibility seriously, even when he didn't always recognize the weight of it.

When I spoke at my father's funeral, I closed by quoting 2 Timothy 4:7: *"I have fought the good fight, I have finished the race."* The verse continues with *"I have kept the faith,"* but I intentionally left that part out. I wasn't entirely sure how much faith my father held at the very end, and I refused to be a hypocrite by adding words that may not have been true for him. In that omission, I felt I honored him more honestly than I ever could have by pretending certainty where there was none.

Funerals usually bring families together, at least briefly. That was not the case here. My father's funeral did not bring my sisters and me any closer at all. In fact, shortly after the service, I remember hugging one of my sisters and telling her that I loved her. She did not respond. In true Goggins fashion, I knew in that moment it would be the last time I ever said those words to her.

Two days after the funeral, while the entire family was still in town, my sisters got together for dinner. I was not invited. That hurt more than I care to admit, especially because I had never done anything to them. The only thing I had ever done that seemed to offend or anger them was simply being born. Not long after that, I stopped trying. Sometimes distance isn't chosen out of anger—it's chosen out of self-preservation.

When I say *"my sisters,"* I do not mean Marina. She has always been a true sister to me, unwavering and present. Though my father tried to reconcile the past during his final days on earth, there were rifts and fractures that remained unresolved. I know my sisters' treatment of me is rooted in something far deeper than anything I did, but if they were to look at it honestly, I had nothing to do with whatever they believe was taken from them.

Once again, that division traces back to the way my father put together his family. I, too, have a fragmented family when it comes to my own children. But I made a promise to myself early on: as long as I am their father, they will never be *"half"* siblings. They are simply brothers and sisters—nothing more, nothing less. I know my life will end before theirs, and I refuse to leave them a world where they are disconnected from one another.

My father left a legacy. That wake and funeral were a celebration of it—complex, imperfect, loud, fractured, and unforgettable. Just like him.

Chapter 17

The Tape Recorder in My Head

My father used to tell me during his lectures, "*You may not be listening to me now, but everything I say is being recorded on a tape recorder inside your head, and one day your mind is going to play it back when you need it.*" As a teenager, I used to roll my eyes every single time he said that. I was convinced he was just lecturing to hear himself talk, filling the air with words I had no interest in absorbing. However, since his death, that tape recorder has played back more times than I can count. His voice, his lessons, and his warnings have surfaced during moments when I least expected them but needed them the most.

Shortly—and I do mean *shortly*—after my father died, I learned that my daughter Kayla was pregnant. She was only seventeen years old, and the weight of that revelation hit me like a ton of bricks dropped without warning. In an instant, I felt anger, confusion, disappointment, acceptance, and fear collide inside me all at once. I remember asking Kayla to meet me at a Starbucks so we could talk, hoping for a calm, focused conversation. Instead, the moment was repeatedly disrupted by phone calls and text messages from my wife at the time, each interruption chipping away at what little emotional balance I was trying to maintain.

She kept asking me what I was going to *do* about the situation, as if there were some clear-cut solution waiting to be imposed. She spoke as though grounding Kayla might magically fix everything, as if discipline alone could rewind time. The truth was far harsher: there was nothing to *"solve."* There was no punishment, no parental decree, no clever maneuver that could undo reality. What I was facing was not a problem with an answer—it was a moment that required wisdom, restraint, and grace.

Just a few months earlier, I had been sitting in a hospital room with my father, listening to him talk about the things he wished he had done differently. He spoke candidly about his regrets as a parent—the moments he wished he had responded with more patience, more understanding, and less reaction. As I reflected on those conversations, it became painfully clear that I was now standing in one of those moments myself. I knew I was in an incredibly delicate situation with my daughter, one that could shape her life—and mine—forever.

I remember sitting quietly with Kayla, studying her face, letting the silence speak before I finally did. I told her that whatever decision she made, I had her back. Those words were not said lightly; they were a promise. Kayla decided to keep the baby, and I made my own decision in response—to help her finish high school and to do everything in my power to ensure she and her child had a quality life. For the first couple of months, the pregnancy seemed to be going well, and I allowed myself a cautious sense of hope.

What I did not realize at the time was how different things were at home when I was not around. Out of sheer desperation, I turned to our church for family counseling, but I handled it poorly. I did not set it up properly; instead, it felt more like an ambush than an act of healing. Looking back, I wish I had approached it with more care and intention. By then, everyone involved was entrenched in their positions, unwilling—or perhaps unable—to move toward one another.

A few weeks later, Kayla moved out. I was devastated by her decision, but I had no choice except to respect it. From that point on, there was a steady and unmistakable deterioration within my household. When I first bought my home, all I wanted was to be there—to enjoy family life, stability, and a sense of belonging. Somewhere along the way, that joy quietly turned into dread.

I would come home after long hours at work and spend hours outside in the yard, finding comfort in physical labor. Neighbors complimented me on having the nicest yard in the neighborhood, and younger guys would ask how I managed to keep it looking so good. I would tell them it was a hobby of mine, but the truth was simpler and sadder: working in the yard beat sitting in a bar, and it gave me a reason not to go inside the house. During the summer, I would sit outside watching CFL football until the final game ended around 12:30 or one o'clock in the morning. It was clear to anyone paying attention that I was not a happy man—I was merely surviving, one long day at a time.

At the same time, I found myself quietly contemplating the next stage of my life. I was on the verge of becoming a grandfather, my children were growing older, and I had four kids who would all be graduating from high school within the next four years. Life felt as though it was accelerating, pushing me forward whether I was ready or not. I had returned to Indiana in 1997 for my children, anchoring my decisions around their needs, their stability, and their future. Now, I was beginning to understand that the season in which they depended on me in the same way was slowly coming to an end.

My kids were starting to make decisions about their own lives, choices that no longer required my constant presence or guidance. That realization was both bittersweet and unsettling. For years, my identity had been rooted in being needed—being the one who showed up, fixed things, and carried the weight. Suddenly, I could see that role changing, and I wasn't sure what was supposed to replace it. At the same time, I was nearing the completion of my PhD, a goal I had worked toward for years with focus and sacrifice.

Professionally, the writing was already on the wall. The college where I worked was experiencing declining enrollment semester after semester, and I knew it was only a matter of time before my position disappeared altogether. I began actively searching for higher education opportunities outside of Indiana, scanning job postings and imagining what a fresh start might look like. One opportunity, in particular, felt almost poetic: an interview in London, Ontario, at a college I had ironically applied to when I was a teenager. Life has a way of circling back on itself like that, offering second chances when you least expect them.

I wasn't just browsing possibilities—I was making real plans to leave Indiana. In my mind, relocation represented reinvention, a chance to start the next chapter with purpose instead of resignation. My wife at the time, however, was reluctant. While I was looking toward what could be, she was holding tightly to what was familiar. That tension between staying and leaving mirrored a much deeper divide, one that would soon make itself impossible to ignore.

It was on June 19, 2015, that my life took its darkest turn. I received the phone call no parent should ever have to answer—the one informing me that my daughter had been shot. In those first moments, I clung desperately to hope, convincing myself that she would survive, that somehow this would not end the way it felt it was going to end. She died before I ever reached the scene. The devastation was immediate and absolute, a kind of shock that leaves you breathing but not living.

As I waited to identify her body, my mind was overwhelmed with thoughts—memories, regrets, unanswered questions, and the cruel finality of what had just happened. One person who carried me through that night was my pastor and dear friend, Chad Temple. I truly do not believe I would have survived those hours without him standing beside me, grounding me when everything else felt unreal. When I finally returned home, I sat in complete silence, surrounded by the familiar walls of a house that suddenly felt foreign. Once I was finally alone, I broke down and cried in a way I never had before.

While I was crying uncontrollably, my wife at the time walked into the room and asked, *"What's wrong now?"* I still don't know exactly what she meant by that question, and I'm not going to use this book to assign her intent. It's possible I misunderstood her in that moment. What I do remember clearly is my response. I looked at her and said, *"I just identified my daughter's body about five hours ago."* That exchange—brief as it was—changed the trajectory of our family forever. Whether I misinterpreted her words or not, the events of those twelve hours altered something inside me that would never fully return to what it had been.

I speak briefly in this book about the beatings I endured as a child, and I know those stories have been told elsewhere— on the international stage and in my brother's book. One thing my father used to tell me was, *"You may have marks on your body from me whipping you, but those will go away. The marks you get from the beatings the world gives you may never go away."* Never had he spoken something so profoundly true. The pain of losing my daughter is a pain my father could never have inflicted upon me. It is the most vicious, unrelenting pain imaginable—the kind that rewires your understanding of suffering altogether.

As if that loss were not enough, my family and I were further wounded by the complete inaction of the Marion County Prosecutor's Office. At the time, the prosecutor was Ryan Mears, and under his leadership, Marion County, Indiana, has been profoundly underserved. Kayla's case was never solved, and we never received so much as a returned phone call despite repeated inquiries. Sadly, we are far from the only family experiencing this kind of silence and neglect.

I have shared my views on politics earlier in this book, but this goes far beyond political affiliation. This is about accountability, compassion, and basic human decency. For the sake of the people of Indianapolis, I genuinely hope change comes. I do not care whether that change comes from a Democrat or a Republican. I hope one day that city elects a prosecutor who truly cares—someone who understands that behind every unanswered case is a family forever trapped in grief.

After the death of my daughter, any plans I had of leaving Indiana were immediately put on hold. Nothing else mattered until I knew my family was stable and cared for. I needed to be present, grounded, and available in whatever way was required, even if it meant setting aside my own ambitions. During that time, I accepted a position at a great community college—one I still work with to this day. What began as an instructional role quickly evolved, and within five years, I moved from instructor to department chair and eventually to a seat on the Chancellor's cabinet.

Professionally, it looked like success. Personally, it felt hollow. Around the same time, my ex-wife, Alicia, and I became co-guardians of Kayla's son, Jadden. That responsibility anchored me even further, and despite the immense challenges, I watched my children continue to succeed and thrive. On the outside, things appeared to be holding together. On the inside, I felt completely empty.

The deterioration of my marriage was intensified by the death of my daughter and by the unilateral decisions I made regarding guardianship of my grandson. Those decisions were made out of necessity and love, but they created fractures that never truly healed. Once the household was stabilized and the immediate crises had passed, my thoughts quietly returned to where they had been before—leaving Indiana and starting again. That idea had never fully left me; it had only been deferred.

My wife at the time, however, had no real desire to go. At the same time, I began to realize that my role on the Chancellor's cabinet was not the direction I wanted to pursue in higher education. I did not want administration to define my career. I wanted to research, to study, to write textbooks, and—most importantly—to teach students. Slowly, and painfully, I came to understand that I had made a significant mistake.

For a long period of time, I had been making decisions based entirely on what everyone else needed, expected, or wanted from me. I had done almost nothing for myself. The weight of that realization was crushing. I remember thinking, more often than I care to admit, that getting hit by a bus might be easier than continuing the life I was living. Those thoughts weren't about wanting to die—they were about wanting the pain and confusion to stop.

During that season, I often reflected on the conversations I had with my father while he was in the hospital. I thought about his regrets, especially his regret of never moving beyond 33 E. Ferry Street. He had told me explicitly to go out and enjoy life as much as possible. Yet here I was, six years after his death, doing the exact opposite. I wasn't enjoying life at all—I was merely enduring it, one obligation at a time.

My decision to change did not come from something my father said, but from something I read. I have always loved presidential biographies—diving into the lives of men who carried enormous power, faced impossible choices, and lived with the consequences of their decisions. I'm fascinated not just by what they accomplished, but by how they justified their choices to themselves. At the time, I was reading a biography of Lyndon B. Johnson, and near the end of the book, there was a moment that stopped me cold.

As Johnson's presidency came to an end and he prepared to leave the White House for Texas, he lit a cigarette. One of his daughters warned him that smoking was going to kill him. His response was simple, direct, and profound. He said, *"I have now raised you girls. I have now been president. Now it's my time."* That sentence landed harder than anything I had read in years. When I placed that moment alongside my father's regrets—the life he wished he had lived more fully—I realized something had to change. I decided it was time for it to be *my* time.

Now, I'll be honest: Lyndon B. Johnson died of a massive heart attack, probably sooner than he should have, and

290 | P a g e

smoking may very well have played a role. But he died on his terms. That distinction mattered to me. From that point forward, I began making decisions on my own terms—decisions that a forty-eight-year-old man doesn't usually make without serious consequences. I didn't like my job, so I quit. I took another position as an instructor at a different college, accepting a substantial pay cut in exchange for alignment with what I actually wanted to do.

I offered one final opportunity for us to leave Indiana together, and when it became clear that wasn't going to happen, I made the decision to leave the marriage. She kept the house, at least temporarily. One thing I will say about my third wife is that she is a remarkable mother and has done great things for Grace. Sometimes people can live under the same roof and still experience completely different lives. That was exactly what happened with us—two people moving in opposite directions while standing in the same place.

I stayed in Indiana briefly, living in an apartment long enough to make sure my kids were acclimated to a new reality. Once they were steady, I eventually moved to Asheville, North Carolina. And remember that young woman I mentioned earlier—Dana Garrett—the one I met at the Brazil movie theater? The one I talked to through the entire movie and still couldn't tell you what we watched? Well, that conversation started back up again, and it never stopped. She is, without question, my best friend.

One of the greatest things about that relationship is knowing she isn't with me for the money. And speaking of money—people going through divorce often say their lawyer fucked them. Well, between my ex-wife's lawyer, my ex-wife, and my own lawyer, I got more than fucked. Dude, they ran a train on me. I will never forget sitting in a virtual mediation, watching my lawyer watch the Johnny Depp trial while she was supposed to be negotiating an equitable settlement on my behalf. Sometimes life just hands you absurdity along with pain.

At the end of the day, none of that mattered as much as one thing: maintaining a solid relationship with my children. That relationship survived. It endured. And that—above everything else—is a victory.

As you know by now, I am doing what I want to do with my life. I have a strong, healthy relationship with my children, and I have a life partner who has proven—time and again—that she is willing to go to battle with me when life demands it. I've written best-selling books, and more importantly, I am intentionally trying to live without regret. That doesn't mean I live without reflection; it means I no longer live paralyzed by the past.

Recently, I returned to Buffalo for a book signing. While I was there, I was honored by the Buffalo City Council, Erie County, and the State of New York for my work as an author and for the contributions to the community made not only by me, but by my father and mother before me. That recognition carried deep meaning—it felt like an acknowledgment that our family's legacy, imperfect as it was, mattered and still mattered.

Skateland, however, told a different story. The building has now been closed for five years. Its decline did not begin with COVID. Poor estate planning quietly started its demise long before the pandemic ever arrived. COVID simply finished it off. Whatever safeguards might have preserved the building were overwhelmed, and the structure was ultimately abandoned. Over time, people broke in and looted anything of value, leaving behind only echoes of what once was.

There was a large sign posted on the door by the City of Buffalo warning that the roof had collapsed and that entering the building was dangerous. In true Goggins fashion, I went inside anyway.

I took pictures of what remained of the skating rink. The mirror ball had fallen from the ceiling. Mold and mushrooms crept across the floor. Water dripped steadily somewhere in the darkness, and I could hear mice—and rats—scurrying through the shadows. As I walked deeper into the building, listening to the cracks and creaks beneath my feet, I couldn't help but think how ironic it would be if the building that gave me so much life ended up taking mine—whether from the floor giving way beneath me or the ceiling collapsing overhead.

I sat there for about thirty minutes, looking around, thinking not only about everything that happened in that building but about my life with my father because of it. It felt as if, at any moment, my father might come and sit beside me. Quite frankly, in that moment, I would have preferred the ghost of my father's presence over anyone else who might have been inside that abandoned space.

I felt sadness watching the building my father built slowly crumble, but I also understood the symbolism. Just like Skateland, his family fractured in ways that could not be undone. And yet, I know that if my father had been given another chance, he would have tried to fix it. Sitting in that building gave me one final lesson from him: legacy does not live in buildings or businesses. Legacy lives in the investment you make in your family. Love builds confidence. Confidence fuels passion. And passion keeps your memory alive long after everything else has fallen apart.

Out of the corner of my eye, I noticed a rat that was far too big for me to want to deal with. Buffalo rats can be monsters. That was my cue—it was time to leave.

At the end of every skating session, my dad used to play Aretha Franklin's *"If You Don't Think."* I pulled out my phone, queued it up, and let the song echo through the empty building one last time in his honor. I could almost hear his voice, just like always, saying, *"Yes baby, it's time to go home!"*

And it was. But home was no longer Buffalo. It wasn't Indianapolis either. Home was Asheville, North Carolina—where my grandson lives with me and Dana, and where my children, though scattered across the country, know they always have a sanctuary. A home built on love. A home built on togetherness.

A home built on the lessons from my father.

Afterword

The Hidden Faces of Domestic Violence: A Personal and Global Reflection

I sincerely hope that you benefit from reading this book. While this sentiment is often expressed, its meaning becomes profoundly different when viewed through the lens of lived experience. One of the most difficult truths to accept is that no one truly knows what takes place behind the closed doors of another person's home. Domestic violence is not confined by geography, culture, or circumstance; it runs rampant across the world, regardless of where one lives or how one appears to the outside world.

I was first struck by this reality while reading a biography of John F. Kennedy, which described the early marriage of his parents, Rose Kennedy and Joseph P. Kennedy Sr. Though their marriage spanned many years and was cloaked in privilege, influence, and public admiration, Rose Kennedy endured profound and sustained emotional abuse. Joseph Kennedy's infidelity was neither discreet nor hidden. He openly brought movie stars into their home, flaunting his affairs in front of his wife. At times, he instructed Rose that she could remain in the house only if she confined herself to a separate area while he carried on his escapades elsewhere.

At one point, Rose reached her breaking point and attempted to leave the marriage, seeking refuge with her family of origin, the Fitzgeralds. Rather than receiving protection or understanding, she was forced to return to the abusive relationship. The message was unmistakable: endurance was expected, even at the expense of personal dignity, emotional safety, and self-worth. The domestic violence Rose Kennedy experienced—though largely invisible to the public—was immeasurable in its psychological toll.

Later in life, Joseph Kennedy suffered a debilitating stroke, rendering him almost entirely dependent on the woman he had long mistreated. Rose became his primary caregiver. Biographers suggest that she did only what was minimally necessary to sustain his life. While his body remained alive, his existence was reduced to mere survival rather than true living. It is difficult not to wonder whether, in this quiet reversal of power, Rose finally reclaimed a measure of justice that had long been denied to her.

This story serves to underscore a critical truth: domestic violence—whether emotional, physical, spiritual, or psychological—knows no boundaries. It recognizes no social class, no race, and no religion. It can exist in households of prominence just as readily as in those of obscurity. The absence of visible bruises does not equate to the absence of harm, and the presence of wealth or status does not protect one from suffering behind closed doors.

Unlike Rose Kennedy, my mother was supported by a strong and unwavering foundation—her parents, Jack O. Gardner and Evelyn Gardner. They stood firmly beside her, not only as parents but as protectors and advocates for her and her two sons. Their presence provided more than shelter; it offered stability, reassurance, and the tangible reminder that she was not alone. Combined with her own resilience and inner strength, this support enabled my mother to overcome her circumstances and ultimately reshape the course of her life.

More recently, I had the profound privilege of developing a friendship with a woman from Hobart, Tasmania, named Twee Shaw. Her story of abuse did not begin in adulthood but in childhood, marking the start of a cycle of violence that spanned generations. Not only was she subjected to abuse, but her mother endured it as well. Their suffering was not limited to the confines of their household; it was compounded by systemic failures at a broader, societal level—failures that allowed such violence to persist without meaningful intervention.

Their story was later shared on my podcast and will also be featured in an upcoming volume of **Stories of Miraculous Transformation**. When I asked Ms. Shaw how she survived such sustained abuse, violence, and injustice, her response was both humbling and illuminating. She did not attribute her survival to a single moment of strength. Instead, she spoke of the resilience her mother modeled, the steady support of her stepfather, and the life-altering intervention by an organization called Engender Equality.

Engender Equality is an Australia-based organization dedicated to helping survivors of domestic violence regain stability, dignity, and independence. Through a comprehensive range of services, the organization provides trauma-informed, evidence-based counselling, advocacy, education, and referral pathways and directs anyone in immediate danger to emergency services. These services are designed not merely to remove victims from danger, but to support long-term restoration—emotionally, socially, and economically.

My mother was fortunate to have parents who were able and willing to provide the resources she needed during her most vulnerable moments. Their support proved critical to her ability to overcome her circumstances and ultimately succeed. However, countless individuals experiencing domestic violence are not afforded such advantages. Many suffer in silence without access to family support, financial stability, or community resources that could offer them a path forward.

Like Rose Kennedy, many victims feel trapped within abusive environments—believing that escape is impossible or fearing the consequences of leaving more than the harm of staying. For some, this sense of entrapment persists for a lifetime; for others, the situation ends only in tragedy. The absence of support systems often transforms abuse from a temporary crisis into a permanent condition.

My conversation with Twee Shaw about her life and her experience with Engender Equality profoundly influenced me. It compelled me to draw upon my own life experiences not only to inform readers but to create a tangible avenue of support for those who are currently suffering. Awareness alone is not enough; action must accompany understanding.

For this reason, one dollar from every purchase of this book is donated directly to Engender Equality to support their mission to rescue and restore victims of domestic violence. This contribution represents more than a financial gesture— it is an intentional effort to transform personal narrative into practical assistance, ensuring that those in crisis have a place to turn when safety, hope, and opportunity feel out of reach.

This book is not intended to benefit only a single organization. If you are reading this work and are involved with an organization dedicated to supporting victims of domestic violence, I invite you to reach out through the Veritas Publishing House website. I would welcome the opportunity to discuss how this book might also serve your mission. Collaboration, when rooted in shared purpose, has the potential to extend hope and resources to individuals who might otherwise remain unseen.

Through the assistance of Engender Equality, Twee Shaw was able to break free from the grip of domestic violence. With access to critical resources and sustained support, she rebuilt her life, created a safe, loving home for her son, and emerged as a highly successful entrepreneur in Tasmania. Her journey stands as a powerful testament to what is possible when survivors are met with compassion, structure, and opportunity rather than silence or indifference.

I do not believe that I—or this book—can single-handedly end domestic violence across the world. Such a challenge is far greater than any one voice or volume. However, I do know this: the cycle of violence has ended within the Goggins family. That truth carries profound significance. Breaking even one generational cycle represents meaningful progress and affirms that change, while difficult, is possible.

I am honored to stand as a warrior alongside survivors like Ms. Shaw and the many advocates who refuse to accept violence as inevitable. Organizations such as Engender Equality serve as steadfast allies in this fight—working tirelessly to rescue, restore, and empower individuals who deserve safety, dignity, and the freedom to rebuild their lives. Together, these efforts form a collective resistance against abuse and a shared commitment to hope.

10-year-old me working at Skateland

The only family picture I have of Mom, Dad, David, and me

Dad in the Vermillion Room

He loved Grace.

Grace is my daughter with Down Syndrome

Dad's Rolls-Royce that I drove in his funeral

www.ingramcontent.com/pod-product-compliance
Lightning Source LLC
Chambersburg PA
CBHW010938120626
46554CB00008B/2511